WOMEN IN GREECE
AND ROME

THE IMAGE OF WOMAN

THE IMAGE OF WOMAN

VERENA
ZINSERLING

WOMEN IN GREECE AND ROME

ABNER SCHRAM
NEW YORK

DISTRIBUTED BY UNIVERSE BOOKS,
NEW YORK

Translated from the German by L. A. Jones

ABNER SCHRAM
1860 Broadway, New York, N. Y. 10023, U.S.A.

Published in the United States of America in 1973
by Abner Schram
(A Division of Schram Enterprises)

© 1972 by Edition Leipzig

Library of Congress Catalog Card Number: 72-91539

Printed in the German Democratic Republic

CONTENTS

INTRODUCTION

Clytemnestra murders her husband, Agamemnon.
She avenges the murder of her daughter Iphigenia.
Electra becomes an accomplice in the murder of Clytemnestra her mother.
Medea, the woman of Colchis who fled to Greece, slays her children.
In one night the women of Lemnos slay their husbands.
Antigone does not slay, but is put to death because of her brother.
Phaedra's passion for her stepson destroys her.
And Jocasta, too, wife and mother of Oedipus, puts a violent end to her life.

Everywhere sorrow pervades the female roles created by the Greek tragedians, who are also the heirs of Homer. What is missing are his sympathetic figures like the self-assured and kindly Queen of Phaeacia and her daughter, who, since they were not raised as Greeks, can meet the castaway Odysseus on a footing of equality—even superiority. By the time of Aeschylus, the destruction of the old order has long been complete. The Trojan War, which began as a degrading quarrel for possession of a beautiful woman, has broken into every relationship. And woman is the loser: her favourable position vis a vis the man in the matriarchal *gens*, or "clan" crumbles away as property and state take shape and have to be defended with force.

"The overthrow of mother-right was the world historical defeat of the female sex. The man took command in the home also; the woman was degraded and reduced to servitude, she became the slave of his lust and a mere instrument for the production of children. This degraded position of the woman, especially conspicuous among the Greeks of the heroic and still more the classical age, has gradually been palliated and glossed over, and sometimes clothed in milder form; in no sense has it been abolished."

(Friedrich Engels, *The Origin of the Family, Private Property and the State*.)

Woman's subjection does not, however, deprive her entirely of significant representation in the arts. In the classical tragedies, which are concerned with fundamental human problems such as guilt and destiny, subjugation and freedom of the individual, we find tragic heroines (often legendary or mythological) acting out of a specifically female motivation. Comedy, perhaps stimulated by an underground emancipation movement arising from the social theories of the sophists, puts woman on the stage in a contemporary setting. However, she is portrayed as an ideal creature—half feminine charm, half masculine "virtue"—acting with a freedom denied her in real life.

Family life is represented in the graphic and plastic arts. Traces of a peaceful existence of unassuming modesty are to be found in scenes painted on vases in bas relief and large mural. Perhaps typically, the contentment of family life is usually banished to the carved tombstone in honour of the dead; there it is ennobled with the breath of a gentle melancholy—an impressive picture acting as a magical preservation and a categorical imperative for those that come after.

Gay and vain, the "friends" of the goddess of love, the *hetaerae*, enjoy lively voluptuous intercourse with a man, and giving up matrimonial virtue and its social recognition keep open for the female sex a narrow path to the masculine world, which means property and power, spirit and enjoyment.

Sappho's song was the song to the beloved maiden. Did she view her unrequited passion as a revolutionary experiment, as the struggle for an emancipation that was never to be realized, shaped in a halfconscious presentiment of the degradation to come?

In the Hellenistic period the narrow bounds of the *polis* are broken and women enter the glare of public attention: as queens, mistresses, philosophers, poetesses. They appear suddenly alongside the simple woman of the people, who for centuries had enjoyed only the freedom which the necessity of selling her labour power—or her whole person, if she was a slave—had brought her.

In early Rome, woman had no right in law to dispose of her own life or property. She was subject to the *patria potestas*, the power of her father, husband, brother: still, she was respected in the community and was often not without influence in political affairs.

The heroines of the Roman myths, who devote or even sacrifice their lives to the common weal by deliberate choice, exhibit a trace of historical realism which may well have approximated to the actual situation of the Roman aristocratic lady. The living image is projected into tradition far otherwise than in Greek art. The literary figure, especially in historiography, reflects a free application of the past to the present—contemporary action was often motivated by old myths—that is characteristic of all Roman politics and art.

The hard, centuries-long class-struggle in Roman society allotted to the woman of the upper strata functions which she was able to exercise in accordance with her personal capabilities: politician and intriguing factionalist, or merely the passive link in a chain of political alliances.

The imperial age begins with the stern marriage laws of Augustus, an attempt, foredoomed to failure, to stabilize the family once more as the germ-cell of the state. But the dissolution of the self-sufficient Roman *familia* was not to be halted. It went hand in hand with Rome's transformation into an empire, which bore but a superficial resemblance to that simple ancient civilization which had only existed centuries before Rome's rise to world domination.

The key to the relations of power as between man and woman is, as in all other things, private ownership. The greater the economic independence of the woman becomes, the more emancipated is she in all spheres of life. Naturally this increase in social power has always been limited by the law and has only held good for the upper and middle classes.

The great range of female professions found in inscriptions allows us to conjecture the part played by women in production, in public and private life, despite the basic servitude of woman, the prototype of all the forms of servitude that charactericed ancient society, its history and culture.

complete destruction of the places, probably at the hands of invaders from the continent or through earthquakes, and another less vigorous period of reconstruction.

It was only at the beginning of the present century that Cretan culture was rediscovered thanks to the pioneering excavations of the Englishman, Sir Arthur Evans. He not only succeeded in bringing to light a buried world, kept alive on frescoes, carved stones and vase decorations, but also revealed the complicated picture of the palace of Cnossos, the labyrinth of the mythical King Minos, and thus made possible the first conclusions about the social relations of the island. The linear B tablets discovered by Evans have thrown little light on social and political aspects of Minoan culture, since these writings have been found to consist entirely of accounts and business records. Much remains unexplained and there is little prospect of closing the important gaps. How far the priest-kings of Cnossos and Phaestos ruled independently of one another, how the lesser vassals divided power and the administration of the island among themselves must for the time being remain open questions. Enjoying the protection of the sea, the island appears to have been scarcely threatened by external enemies, the palaces are not fortified, not equipped for defence.

Let us return to the curly-headed Ariadne. In the myth she plays a most decisive part: it is her ball of thread on which everything depends. Her historical sisters seem to have played a hardly less significant role. The numerous representations of women in the island's art reveal not only their dress and appearance but their situation in society as well. Next to the king sat the queen. She lived in the luxurious rooms of the palace, tended her beauty in warm baths, took pleasure in the colourful fauna and flora of the murals, strolled in courts and loggias, or retired to the subdued light of her many-storied living quarters.

But above all she was the priestess of the great goddess and this is the principal way she is presented to us on carved stones and frescoes. This mother-godhead, who as sea, mountain and tree goddess, as mistress of the animal world, as the naked embodiment of life and love, as mother of the divine child rules over men and nature, is the image of the Cretan woman written large. Her cult reflects the important role played by the woman in Cretan society, which in all probability had matriarchal features. Above all, women are in the service of the goddess, handle the holy symbols, make sacrifices and worship. The cult ceremonies, which may have been performed in the open palace court, among other places, were clearly great public events. Terraced stands for the spectators, upon which the elegant ladies shown in of Cnossos miniature frescoes sat, have been found again.

The Cretan women wore the short-sleeved bodice, open to the waist and exposing the breasts, and the long, many-coloured, probably brilliantly embroidered flounced skirt. Their black hair is curled in ringlets underneath a jewelled headband above the brow and falls in single locks on shoulders and back. Priestesses lead the cult dance, also wearing the many-coloured, very low-cut dress.

Perhaps the bull-game was the climax of the festival. At any rate Cretan girls also took part in this deadly dangerous entertainment, wearing only a skirt and rich ornaments on arms and neck.

The participants had to seize the bull by the horns and turn a somersault to clear the animal's back.

Replicas in faience of women's clothes, of girdles and knotted sashes and seals which represent a woman with the holy double-edged axe and a skirt in her hands, have given rise to the conjecture that by wearing a special cult dress it was possible for a mortal woman to take upon herself the role of the goddess. Whether the image, in the shape of the famous snake-priestess of the palace of Cnossos, is a priestess or queen dressed up as such, or whether she represents the great goddess herself in the form of a cult-statuette, is a riddle, but at any rate she is the perfect embodiment of the beautiful Cretan woman. She demonstrates the ideal of full feminine lines—a narrow waist and round hips. The dress allows the figure to appear at its most advantageous: again the narrow bodice, the bare breasts, the tightly-laced waist, the long, flounced skirt and a skirt-like apron over the abdomen. Sometimes the skirt is divided like a trouserskirt, and a large bow adorns the neck. Probably the choice of materials, patterns and trimmings and the jewelry reflected the wealth and taste of the individual wearer. The elegant, socially important Cretan lady was to become in many ways the pattern for her Grecian sister on the Peloponnese. Just as we today look to the great cities of the world for elegance and haute couture, so for the ladies of Mycenae and Tiryns, Crete was the home of refinement and taste. But borrowing was not done indiscriminately—changes were made and a new style created.

From the beginning of the second millennium, the Achaeans were in occupation of Greece. They had taken possession of it by force of arms and subjugated the population they found there. The Achaeans brought with them to Greece their own characteristic type of house, the *megaron*—consisting of an open vestibule leading to two rooms, one lying behind the other; in the main room was the hearth, the heart of the construction. Grey-black monochrome pottery and the simple bronze tools which have been found betray a low level of culture.

In the sixteenth century, at the time of the New Palaces in Crete, powerful princely centers arose on the Greek mainland. The most important was Mycenae, which lay 9 miles inland from the coast in Argolis; Mycenae was to give its name to the next four centuries of the pre-Hellenic era. Other important centers were Tiryns, the Messinian Pylos of Homer's Nestor, Orchomenus in Boeotia and the Acropolis of Athens. Unlike the unfortified palaces of Crete, the royal Mycenaean residences are surrounded by stout walls, in some cases having a breadth of up to 33 feet (as at Tiryns), so that the Greeks of aftertime took them for the work of the Cyclops on account of the gigantic dimensions of the stone blocks fitted together without mortar. These fortresses and the rich finds of weapons in graves proclaim the warlike character of Mycenaean society. The military kings had considerable power over the peasants, who settled around their fortresses and who, like their followers living in the lower town, had to take part in campaigns often lasting years. The 'Iliad' is the epic tale of such a warlike adventure undertaken by the Mycenaean Prince Agamemnon and his Achaean allies. In this warlike, seafaring, trading world of men, the Achaean lady had to fill the leading position in the house, to supervise family and slaves and administer the household, during her husband's long absences. It is these demands of daily life that explain the harsher character of the Achaean woman, who has not come down to us in many plastic representations, as compared with the Cretan.

We see women hunting on their own, two of them standing on the platform of the chariot and holding the reins. We meet the Achaean lady at the dangerous boar-hunt, intercepting the boar with her javelin. But even the woman of Mycenae had an eye for feminine elegance and the splendours of fashion. In addition to the traditional shirt-like robe, richly worked with gold embroidery, the Achaean lady wore Cretan dress.

Minoan inspiration is everywhere to be seen, above all in the fields of art and fashion. It is sometimes difficult to tell indigenous from imported products, so strong was Cretan influence. As against Cretan masterpieces the Achaeans did not abandon their own tradition and feeling for style; in many respects they adapted the Cretan inspiration to their own Achaean taste. This accounts for the proportions of the gigantic ornaments of gold and precious stones such as the golden eardrops, adorned with rosettes, 3 inches in diameter, and the silver brooches with golden decorations $8\frac{1}{2}$ inches in length, or the massive toothed diadems of hammered gold foil. Cretan delicacy had given place to Achaean monumentality.

As in Crete women seem to have exercised important functions in the cult. Drawn up in processional lines they stride to the ceremonial sacrifice on the frescoes of Tiryns and Thebes or look down from a balcony upon a cult ceremony. In warlike Mycenae the Cretan snake-goddess appears as a shield-goddess, who because of her protection of palace and ruler has been seen as a precursor of the Greek Athena. Women also participated in the ceremonies of her cult, as a limestone slab found in Mycenae shows. In addition to the gods Zeus, Hera and Dionysus mentioned on Linear B tablets from Pylos, the worship of a divine child brought up by two mothers or nurses, was important. This is the interpretation given of the ivory group, found at Mycenae, of two seated women, joined by a sort of cloak, who together are holding a child on their knees.

In the twelfth century, disaster overtook Mycenaean civilisation, which fell a victim to tribes conquering Greece from the north. But the Mycenaean sense of form remained alive in local traditions for centuries.

THE TROJAN WAR AND AFTER

After the brilliant Mycenaean epoch had been brought to an end by invasions from the north, the civilisation of the whole Aegean area sank to the level of simple peasant life. The existing population was partly subjugated by its culturally inferior conquerors, partly assimilated, partly driven away to find new homes. In the final settlement areas of the main Greek tribes, Dorians and North-Western Greeks, Ionians and Aeolians, the beginnings of the later city or *polis* civilization appeared. Owing to the more or less considerable isolation of the various districts from one another, *polis* creation and cultural development proceeded at varying speeds in different places.

Not all regions of the homeland were visited by the "Dorian invasion": Attica especially, colonized by Ionians, was able to fend off the invaders and become the centre of a new civilization. From the eleventh to the eighth century B.C., pottery reflected a lessening of the Mycenaean tradition, the world of shapes as observed in and copied from nature giving place to a strong linear, geometrical ornamentation on artistically perfect vessels.

The creation of the *polis* was based on a social differentiation which had already begun in the eleventh century at the beginning of the geometrical period (so named for the style of its pottery). In the course of the archaic period (named for the pottery of the 7th and 6th centuries) these trends continued, resulting in the gradual consolidation of the typically Greek form of the state— the city-state. A section of free peasants became impoverished and sank into dependence upon rich landowners. Some drifted into the towns and formed there the new stratum of traders and artisans, who with increasing prosperity took up the struggle for political and social rights against the land-owning aristocracy in power in the *poleis*. The towns soon grew rapidly without a corresponding development of the productive forces. The result was the impoverishment of a large part of the population and social unrest—the only solution was to emigrate. Many Greek city-states encouraged emigration in order to control their overpopulation and at the same time to extend their trading area. In the 8th century, the first colonies were founded on Sicily and in South Italy until, with the colonization of the Black Sea in the 6th century, when the Greeks were sitting around the Mediterranean coast "like frogs around the pond" *(Plato)*.

But even colonization was no panacea for the deep class antagonisms which had broken out between the aristocracy and the people, or *demos*. The *demos* were manipulated by individual aristocrats, who, in the guise of representing the people, usurped power and ruled as tyrants maintaining, meanwhile, sumptuous courts (Cypselos and Periander in Corinth, Peisistratus and his sons in Athens, Polycrates on the island of Samos). They failed to establish lasting dynasties, however, and by the end of the archaic period, almost all the Greek cities had returned to an aristocratic or democratic form of government.

The period whose main lines of development have been presented here in rough outline covered more than five centuries.

In the dark centuries of the early geometrical epoch, characterized by the chaos of war, we search in vain for traces of the lives of women. They have disappeared with the remnants of a modest peasant civilization. It is only in the two great Homeric epics that women appear, but here in the shadow of a masculine world of warfare and heroism. Homer's epics preserve the great Mycenaean past, his heroes spring from a long-deceased race of men, whose shadowy outlines the poet filled with the flesh and blood of his own times. We no longer have the Achaean woman of the Mycenaean castles, but the Greek woman of the 8th–7th centuries who bears only the name of her mythical ancestor. Her mode of life, however, is little changed, since the chivalric ideals of the late geometrical period were the same in all essentials as those of the Mycenaean lords more than four centuries earlier. Basically it is true of all the female figures of the 'Iliad' that they have no function as active individuals carrying the plot forward. Their lives are more or less passive, being woven into the destinies of the men. Even the destructively beautiful Helen, for whose sake the hosts of Achaeans and Trojans confront one another, only plays the part of a woman induced and seduced by Aphrodite. She sits at home:

"An ample web magnificent she wove,
  Inwrought with numerous conflicts for her sake
  Beneath the hands of Mars endured by Greeks
  Mail-arm'd, and Trojans of equestrian fame."

W. Cowper   *(Iliad 3, 125—127)*

then, at the behest of Iris, messenger of the Gods,
  "... she shrouded herself in a veil of shimmering silver,
  Hastened away from the house with teardrops
  secretly falling.

Yet was she never alone, two serving girls followed after,
  Swiftly she came to the place where the Scaian Gate towered upwards"   *(3, 141—145)*

There she meets the Trojan King Priam, whom she approaches "in fear and trembling," but then shows herself to be very knowledgeable and clever at pointing out the Achaean heroes, whom the two watch from the tower. In the 'Iliad' there is comparatively little said about family organization and the life of women, but enough to round out the picture: King Priam is the head of a gigantic family. Together with his wife Hecuba, who has presented him with 19 sons, several "women of the palace" have shared in the procreation of the other 31. "Fifty sons did I call mine when the Danai came", cries Priam with pride in his lament for his favourite son, Hector. All his sons and his daughters live with their families in

"... Priam's palace, built
  With splendid porticoes, and each within
  Had fifty chambers lined with polish'd stone,
  Contiguous all, where Priam's sons reposed
  And his sons' wives, and where, on the other side,
  In twelve magnificent chambers also lined
  With polish'd marble and contiguous all,
  The sons-in-law of Priam lay beside
  His spotless daughters, ..."

W. Cowper   *(6, 242—250)*

Hecuba as queen exercised supervision over the household and the performance of sacrifices to the gods. Before going into battle, Hector charges her:
  "Thou, therefore, gathering all our matrons, seek
  The fane of Pallas, huntress of the spoil,
  Bearing sweet incense; but from the attire
  Treasured within thy chamber, first select
  The amplest robe, most exquisitely wrought,
  And which thou prizest most,—then spread the gift
  On Athenaean Pallas' lap divine.
  Twelve heifers also of the year, untouch'd
  With puncture of the goad, promise to slay
  In sacrifice, if she will pity Troy,
  Our wives and little ones, ..."

W. Cowper   *(6, 269—276)*

"He ceased; the Queen, her palace entering, charged
  Her maidens; they, incontinent, throughout

All Troy convened the matrons, as she bade.
Meantime into her wardrobe incense-fumed,
Herself descended; there her treasures lay,
Works of Sidonian women, whom her son
The godlike Paris, when he cross'd the seas
With Jove-begotten Helen, brought to Troy.
The most magnificent, and varied most
With colours radiant, from the rest she chose
For Pallas; vivid as a star it shone,
And lowest lay of all. Then forth she went,
The Trojan matrons all following her steps.
But when the long procession reach'd the fane
Of Pallas in the heights of Troy, to them
The fair Theano open'd the portals wide,
Daughter of Cisseus, brave Antenor's spouse,
And by appointment public, at that time,
Priestess of Pallas. All with lifted hands
In presence of Minerva wept aloud.
Beauteous Theano on the Goddess' lap
Then spread the robe, and to the daughter fair
Of Jove omnipotent her suit address'd."

W. Cowper   (6, 286—304)

But one of the young women of the palace is overtaken by a heartrending destiny, Andromache, Hector's young wife, who struggles in vain to save the life of her husband, fighting a senseless heroism by opposing to it helplessness and the human duty to guard the future of her small son. But—and how could it be otherwise?—she receives an answer summoning her to show a dutiful obedience:

"Go then, and occupy content at home
The woman's province; ply the distaff, spin
And weave, and task thy maidens. War belongs
To man; ..."

W. Cowper   (6, 490—492)

In the same way she is the last to be told the terrible news of Hector's death, for

"She in a closet of her palace sat,
A twofold web weaving magnificent,
With sprinkled flowers inwrought of various hues,
And to her maidens had commandment given
Through all her house, that compassing with fire
An ample tripod, they should warm a bath
For noble Hector from the fight return'd."

W. Cowper   (22, 440—444)

In a torment of terror
"... she rush'd with palpitating heart
And frantic air abroad, by her two maids
Attended; soon arriving at the tower,
And at the throng of men, awhile she stood
Down-looking wistful from the city-wall,
And, seeing him in front of Ilium, dragg'd
So cruelly toward the fleet of Greece,
O'erwhelm'd with sudden darkness at the view
Fell backward, with a sigh heard all around.
Far distant flew dispersed her head-attire,
Twist, frontlet, diadem, and even the veil
By golden Venus given her ..."

W. Cowper   (22, 460—470)

In the 'Odyssey' we meet Penelope, the wife of the "noble sufferer" Odysseus, a female character whose situation is equally difficult, but who is able to triumph by virtue of her confidence and intelligence. Whereas in the 'Iliad' the destinies of the men are fulfilled in battle, the epic that succeeds it two generations after takes us into the royal household of Odysseus, who after the end of the Trojan war is driven about the world and has to undergo terrible ordeals before he can return to Ithaca after twenty years' absence. Penelope is believed to be a widow, and her growing son Telemachus begins to grow into the role of master of the house and to assume the responsibility for his mother's destiny.

"But come now, go to thy bower, and deal with such
things as ye can
With the rock and the loom be busy, and thine
handmaids order and teach,
That they speed the work and the weaving: but for
men is the word and the speech;
For all, but for me the chiefest, for here am I the
might and the power."

W. Morris   (Odyssey 1, 356—359)

Here the bounds of authority are laid down: the woman gives orders in the house but otherwise must obey the master of the house—even when he is her own son. Had Penelope been able to bring herself to abandon her marital fidelity and to wed one of her besieging suitors, this would only have been possible with the consent of her father,
"... that he should affiance his daughter and
give her to him who pleased him best." (2, 53—54)

Of course, as master of the house Telemachus had the power to send his mother back to his grandfather. If he had done so, Penelope's father would have had to pay a high indemnity. A bride was bought from her father at the cost of rich presents, which would have had to be returned in the event of a divorce. Even the woman herself was wooed with gifts, which the suitors have brought to Penelope:

"And each man sent his henchman the gifts thereto
  to bear.
For Antinous thither brought he a great robe
  wondrous fair;
All 'broidered, with twelve brooches thereon all
  wrought of gold,
And every one well-fitted with hooks well-wrought
  to hold.
For Eurymachus a collar of gold most deftly done,
All hung about with amber that shone out as the
  sun.
And the swains of Eurydamas brought him two
  earrings wrought full fair,
Three-beaded; and great glory from out them
  glittered there.

And the henchman of Pisander, Polyctor's son the king,
Brought up with him a neck-chain, a fair and seemly thing;
And each one of the Achaeans for fair gifts to give her sent."

W. Morris   (18, 292—301)

Penelope, however, evades them all. For many years she deceives her suitors by means of a trick which significantly harmonizes with her most important task. She weaves a sheet as shroud for the husband who is presumed dead, and will not marry before it is finished. But it will never be finished, for at night she unravels the work she has done by day. Thus she spends her time in the women's quarters—rooms shut off in the upper story of the house—commands her fifty maid servants and holds the key to the store rooms, in which stand chests full of clothes and costly weapons. If a guest is expected, Penelope takes a bath, chooses "fresh robes", goes down to the lower rooms and receives him as the mistress of the house. She has a relationship of confidence with some of her servants, as with Eurycleia, Odysseus'

Penelope at her loom

old nurse, the embodiment of affection and faithfulness, and also in former times with the unfaithful Melantho, whom she had herself brought up lovingly. Odysseus' nurse is an early representation of the confidante character, who is not brought into the story for her own sake but as the worldly-wise, unswervingly loyal companion of the hero or heroine. The nurse—who is often portrayed in later times, as a slave or a woman of the common people —is permitted by the intimacy of the relationship to lavish on her favourite well-meant warnings, the service of love, and an abundance of common sense. Eurycleia remains faithful to her foster child Odysseus over many years; her loyalty extends to the entire household. She warns young Telemachus:

"O child, and might'st thou do it to take on thee
    good heed,
And keep the house with wisdom and ward well all
    the gear!"

W. Morris   (19, 22—24)

She herself sketches the basic features in her character when she answers the returning Odysseus, whom she, significantly enough, has been the first to recognise:

"O me, my child! what a word from the hedge of
    thy teeth hath sped!
Thou knowest my will, how steadfast, how little
I use to bend;
I will hold me hard as the iron or some stark stone
to the end."

W. Morris   (19, 492—494)

But the reader is not only taken in the 'Odyssey' into the household of Odysseus himself; other houses of Greek nobles open their doors to receive the wandering father or the searching son. Telemachus comes upon a wedding feast in the house of the Spartan King Menelaus. His wife, Helen, takes part with ease in the conversation of the men, leaving her women's quarters with the implements of her handwork to do so.

"And there with her came Adraste, who set forth the
    well-wrought chair;
But the carpet of soft wool woven forth did Alcippe
    bear,
And Phylo a silver basket, the gift of Polybus' wife
Alcandra . . .
And his wife to Helen moreover gave goodly gifts
and great:

A distaff of gold and a basket fashioned on wheels
to run,
Of silver wrought; but its edges about with gold
were done.
And e'en this it was that was carried and set down
by Phylo the maid,
With the wrought yarn all fulfilled, and the distaff
over it laid,
Reached out therefrom, with its head well charged
with dark-blue wool.
So Helen sat in the chair and under her feet was the
stool."

W. Morris   (4, 123—136)

A similarly respected position is enjoyed by the self-possessed Arete, Queen of the Phaeacians, who "sits and spins the purple threads" in the palace among her maids, and next to her is the throne of her lord. She is hospitably concerned to make Odysseus welcome and orders

". . . her handmaidens to heed
And get the three-foot caldron on the fire in haste
and speed.
So the great three-foot bath-feeder they set on the
fire to stand,
And therein they poured the water and thereunder
laid the brand;
And the flame licked the caldron's belly and warm
the water grew.
Meanwhile, for the guest Arete from the chamber
brought thereto
A chest exceeding goodly, and therein for him to have
She laid the gold and the raiment which those
Phaeacians gave;"

W. Morris   (8, 433—440)

Nausicaa, the young daughter of the Phaeacian king, is the embodiment of the beautiful, virtuous and prudent girl who prepares herself for marriage in obedience to her parents and the gods. In the 7th century a fixed convention had obviously grown up concerning the qualities which constituted womanly virtue. But the estimate is always made from a masculine point of view. Women are weak, not only physically but also morally, and it is better for the man to treat them with circumspection and look to his own interests. These tones are already evident in Homer and never die away throughout the whole ancient world.

Cult dance of youths and girls

Hesiod, whose heart is in the life and work of the small peasant in remote Boeotia, a world far different from Homer's, takes up the theme of women and blows up his criticism into real tirades of hatred against the fair sex:

"Neither let the scarlet woman beguile thee with
wheedling words, aiming at thy barn. Who putteth
his trust in a woman putteth his trust in a
deceiver."

A. W. Mair   (*Theogony, 591—602*)

The Samian Semonides (c. 600 B.C.), though deriving from Hesiod, outdoes the latter in point of bitterness and nastiness in the characterization of feminine qualities. The various types of women, he says, are descended from swine, fox, dog, ass, weasel, horse and monkey and have adopted their characteristic features, whereby they of course plague that noble creature, man, unless he has the luck to get hold of one of the rare hard-working "busy bees." And even then the goodly Ionian groans, it still is a woman: "for Zeus created this the greatest of all evils—women."

Here is a taste of Semonides' rhetoric:

"At the creation God made women's natures
various. One he made from a bristly sow:
and all her household welters in confusion,
lying aground in miscellaneous muck,
while she unwashen in unlaundered clothes
reposes in her pigsty, fattening.
God made another from a canny vixen,
the woman who knows all—nothing escapes her,

evil and good, she knows it all alike.
Many a time she says an evil thing,
but often good: such is her shifty nature."

Gilbert Highet   (*Fragment 7*)

These verses of classification, however, convey an attitude that is not typical of the early Greek lyric. Archilochus of Paros, its earliest and most personal representative, sings of Neobule, his affianced bride:

"Ah were it only granted me to take Neobule's hand!

J. A. Symonds   (*Fragment 71*)

"Holding a myrtle-rod she blithely moved,
And a fair blossoming rose; the flowing tresses
Shadowed her shoulders falling to her girdle.
(Her hair perfumed with myrrh and oh! a breast
would make a greybeard yearn.)"

J. A. Symonds   (*Fragments 25/26*)

Who this homage was intended for, is hidden for ever. The choral songs of Alcman from Sardis (second half of the 7th century B.C.), sung and danced to by a Spartan group of girls in honour of Artemis Orthia, also possess this personal element. Probably there had been a dialogue between poet and chorus so that many parts of the songs were improvised, which explains their freshness and liveliness. They give the names of the individual singers and praise each of them in affectionate comparisons. Beautiful Agido is the star among the ten maidens but the hair of the choral leader

"Hagesichora shines like purest gold
And her silvery countenance—why do I talk so much?
Here is Hagesichora herself!"   *(Fragment 1)*

SAPPHO

Nowhere is the elegant, exclusive life of women caught with such poignancy as in the poems of the "tenth of the nine muses"—the poetess Sappho. For the first time we hear the voice of a woman speaking about her sex. She stands upon a lonely peak in the ancient world, but by the fifth century successors had appeared in Boeotia— Corinna of Tanagra and Myrtis, who is said to have challenged Pindar.

Sappho lived about 600 B.C. near the Lydian Empire, at Mytilene on the island of Lesbos, was of aristocratic descent, was married and had one daughter. In public life she was in charge of a girls' school, a *thiasos*. In Lesbos and probably at other places in Greece there were several such boarding-schools, in which the young girls of well-to-do families lived together under the supervision of well-educated, experienced women. They spent their days performing cult rituals in the service of the love-goddess, Aphrodite. But they also received instruction in singing, dancing and poetry, learnt the rules of social etiquette, good taste, knowledge and sensitivity in the arts of love, practised an instrument, bound garlands of flowers and did handwork; but they were thereby deliberately kept at a distance from political events of their time. When they had finished the training that made Lesbian girls so famous, they had to take leave of Sappho and their schoolmates and turn what they had learnt to practical use in marriage.

For the wedding Sappho composed the wedding song, which the girl-friends of the departing bride performed. Leave-taking from the girl who had to go away with her husband moved Sappho to compose songs in which she bewailed her love and the pain of parting. These personal outpourings enchant by the deep passion expressed in wonderfully vivid comparisons, whose compulsive power is not lost on the modern reader:
"To a Bride.
Blest beyond earth's bliss, with heaven I deem him
Blest, the man that in thy presence near thee
Face to face may sit, and while thou speakest,
    Listening may hear thee,
And thy sweet-voiced laughter:—In my bosom
    The rapt heart so troubleth, wildly stirred:

Let me see thee, but a glimpse—and straightway
    Utterance of word
Fails me; no voice comes; my tongue is palsied;
    Thrilling fire through all my flesh hath run;
Mine eyes cannot see, mine ears make dinning
    Noises that stun;
The sweat streameth down, my whole frame seized with
    Shivering,—and wan paleness o'er me spread,
Greener than the grass; I seem with faintness
    Almost as dead."

Walter Headlam   *(Fragment 31)*

The 20th century reader may be startled by the intensity of passion expressed in this unconventional relationship between a woman and a young girl:
"Love has shaken my senses
Like a wind from the mountain that sweeps through the oak trees"

C. M. Bowra   *(Fragment 47)*

    Love
"Love has unbound my limbs and set me shaking,
    A monster bitter-sweet and my unmaking."

C. M. Bowra   *(Fragment 130)*

It is in no way an intense form of maternal love that Sappho felt for her girls but captivation with the girl's person.

Sappho was not only the great lover but knew also the torments of jealousy and hatred of a rival. Thus she attacked the mistress of another *thiasos*, Andromeda, in her songs, and many of her girls seem to have deserted to the enemy.

Sappho stands at the end of the 7th century, which was marked by strong oriental influences upon Greek culture. Before her she had the Lydian empire with the highly cultured Sardis and she lived in the midst of a lively traffic between the coastal towns of Asia Minor and the Greek islands.

Sappho's songs bring to mind the enchanting statues of maidens which were carved half a century later by Ionian and Attic artists and set up upon the citadel of Athens. They breathe elegance and beauty and the serene cheerfulness of Anacreon's verses with their sparkling, unabashed sensual enjoyment.

The 6th century ended on a note of sophistication in art and life. But the splendour of the tyrants' courts served less the praise of women than the courting of handsome men and boys. Though episodes like that of the wedding of Agariste, daughter of Cleisthenes, tyrant of Sicyon, tell us something about the woman, the tendency towards the lowering of her social status is evident. Despite wide differences in the various Greek city-states she found herself in a society ruled politically by men, whose chief occupation was war, and was thrust into the background, into a closed domestic atmosphere—this at least was the lot of the Greek married woman.

GODDESSES

Before classical times, the power and glory of the Greek goddesses was well established.

In the opinion of Herodotus it was Homer and Hesiod who gave the Greeks their gods. This is undoubtedly correct, but it must be said that in the course of generations their spheres of authority were modified or extended. At the end of the archaic era, however, the basic structure of divine Olympus had taken shape even if later every period invested it with its own notions. The Olympian gods were worshipped differently in different places and often identified with local deities, but a more or less universally accepted range of qualities had evolved.

The "first lady" of Olympus was Hera, consort of the absolute ruler Zeus. She was bound to him in holy wedlock, watched jealously and shrewishly over her lord's marital fidelity and was worshipped as the protectress of marriage. In art she is portrayed as the Homeric Hera with the shining white arms, as the mature, matronly woman.

Her opposite was the warrior-maiden, the motherless daughter of a divine father—Athena. Even in the 'Iliad' she is the goddess of the city whom Hecuba and her women implore to protect them. She is to be found in the thick of battle, succouring the heroes in person. Helmeted, lance in her hand and the *aegis* (shield) with its petrified head of Medusa before her breast—this is how Athena is portrayed in art. She was not only the martial virgin but also the patroness of the arts and crafts. She taught women the art of the loom, men the craft of metal working and pottery and, in Athens, the growing of the olive tree.

As goddess of the hunt and chaste virgin, who in beauty and slimness was Aphrodite's greatest rival, Artemis, the "moon" goddess, took her place in the divine heaven. Originally she had been mainly a deity of death like her bowman brother, Apollo. The stag is associated with her as mistress of the world of animals and plants. She retained qualities of an older fertility goddess and this explains her function as the nativity goddess, and patroness of pregnant women and marriage in general.

Perhaps the most mighty of the Greek goddesses was the one borrowed from the Orient, Aphrodite, whose power could lay the whole world in her chains. The most beautiful of beauties, she received the apple of Paris even if by means of her characteristic cunning. She spurned neither lies nor deceit to obtain her purpose, and this was always love—not the love sanctioned by the bond of marriage, but love that was free, sudden, hot and often wayward. She had been married in heaven to the limping, sooty Hephaestus but only to deceive him with the radiant god of war, Ares. No other goddess played such a part in the lives of women. No woman could afford to get on the wrong side of Cypris, as Aphrodite was called, after the island Cyprus, which was her own particular home—for what was a Greek woman without her gifts—her beauty and seductive art?

Golden chains consisting of stylized plant elements

CLASSICAL PERIOD: WOMEN OF ATHENS

SOCIAL AND LEGAL POSITION OF WOMEN

"If I now mention the women who have become widows, and speak of womanly virtue, I can say all that is needed with a brief exhortation: fulfil diligently the tasks that nature has assigned you and you will be praised; and the highest praise you can win is to be spoken of by men as little as possible, whether for good or ill."   *(Thucydides, II, 45)*

Pericles' funeral oration for those who fell in the Samian war in the summer of 430 B.C. is in many respects a statement of government policy the laying down of official standards and ideals. But this one sentence addressed to the widows of the fallen is interesting for us in several ways: first, it is a succint expression of the Athenian virtue; secondly, it marks out the boundaries within which women of Attic society had to remain, or rather, remain hidden; and lastly it encourages a hard look at the social realities of Athens, particularly in light of such self-serving descriptions as the following:

"Our city in its whole activity is a school and a cultural model for Hellas."   *(Thucydides II, 41)*

In the fifth century Athens was the leading economic, political and cultural force in Greece. Despite devastating wars—the first half of the century was overshadowed by the struggle against the Persians and the second half saw the strength-sapping war with conservative Sparta— nowhere did culture, the arts and the sciences flourish as in Athens. For the history of art the fifth century means the severe style of its second quarter, the buildings on the *Acropolis,* the floruit of the classical style with the work of Pheidias and the monumental treasury of the virgin goddess Athena, the *Parthenon.*

For no other Greek community do we possess nearly as many records about society and art as for Athens. Nowhere do we find so many pieces to fit into the mosaic of everyday life; but it is just the multiplicity and variety of the sources that makes it difficult to establish an authentic historical picture. This holds good for the reconstruction of historical events and the causes of political and artistic development but most of all for the life of women in these ancient times. Above all artists and philosophers were interested less in everyday realities than in the representation of conceptual or artistic ideals. Neither the heroines of classical tragedy nor Aristophanes' female rebels present the Attic woman as she really was. In the schoolmasterly discourses of Plato, Aristotle and Xenophon that concern themselves with the conduct of women, didactic purpose obscures the simple human realities which are the object of our quest. Much more reliable are the static pictures of the vase-paintings or the forensic speeches of Demosthenes or Lysias. Conflicting evidence has given rise to two opposing views in the course of academic research, the one bewailing the dreary bondage of the Athenian woman, the other suggesting that it may not have been as bad as it seemed.

It is true of almost the whole of Greece that the social position of women was decidedly lowered in the classical period. The pervasive politicization of life in the city-state together with the necessary preoccupation of the men with political affairs, for which only they could take the responsibility in time of war, led to a strict separation of male and female duties and interests. The woman's sphere was the house and the family, less as mistress than as servant of the head of the family, her father or husband. The two spheres, the interior one of the woman and the exterior of the man, were not of equal importance; the female sphere was subservient to the male and directed by it.

Even in the house there was a separation of the masculine quarters from the feminine living areas. The women's quarters, the *gynaeconitis*, located in the upper storey, were mostly kept shut and seldom entered by men. There the young girls grew up in the society of their nurses and mothers and were often shyer and more ignorant than was good for them. A respectable married woman went out of her quarters as rarely as possible, since it was thought more decent "if the woman remains at home than if she runs around outside; however, it is more of a disgrace for a man to stay at home than to be abroad, getting on with his business." (*Xenophon, Econ. 7*) Moreover,

"We women can't go out just when we like:
We have to wait upon our men, and wake
The servants, then we put the children straight,
We have to wash and feed them."

(*Aristophanes, Lysistrata 16—19*)

The woman did no shopping but left it to her husband or to slaves. It was only on the occasion of public holidays and family festivals, marriages and funerals that it was seemly for a woman to leave the house, though if one is to believe Aristophanes, visits to female friends and neighbours were possible, even if perhaps regarded with disfavour.

The men's symposia would have been singularly boring without the presence of attractive women, but the behaviour of any Athenian who took it into his head to bring his wife along, would have been considered quite outré. She was equally excluded from the assembly of the people, a visit to the theatre must have been a rarity and on the greatest occasions of Greek life, the pan-Hellenic games, she stayed dutifully at home. It was very rarely that a woman succeeded in being tolerated as a spectator as was the case with Pherenice, who disguised herself as a man and accompanied her son to Olympia as his trainer; she herself came from a famous family of Olympic victors.

Women were not permitted to enter the shrines of the oracles. Nonetheless it was a woman, the Pythia, who in her capacity as priestess of Apollo of Delphi pronounced the oracles, the interpretation of the divine message was of course left to the masculine priesthood, who gained a considerable influence over political events and the individual destinies of men.

The upbringing of the woman was directed from birth onwards towards making her as simple and chaste as possible, ignorant of the arts—few women could read and write—obedient to her male partner and as busy as a bee in the house.

It hardly needs to be said that these strict conventions only applied to the prosperous. The ordinary woman of the people could of course not afford to sit in the interior of the house and hide herself shamefacedly from all the world. She had to work herself to help maintain her family and thus it happened that while distinguished ladies were seldom seen in street or market-place, tradeswomen were everywhere in evidence, offering their wares for sale in public places. Such were the "turnip-cabbage-vegetable-butter-wenches" and the "onion-cheese-baking-bar-maids" to whom Lysistrata directed her appeal. We also encounter the female moneylender and the flower-girl in Aristophanes. Women could work for wages in the wool-preparing and clothes-making trades. Aristotle shows his knowledge of the everyday life of ordinary women when he writes:

"How is it possible to keep the wives of the poor from
going out?" (*Politics, 4, 15 p. 1300a 6 foll.*)
and

"... the poor have to use their wives and
children as servants since they have no slaves."

(*Politics, 6, 8 p. 1323a 5 foll.*)

However the most respected profession for women was that of midwife, who mostly possessed medical knowledge and skill. Every prosperous family had nurses and female attendants, who also came from the lower classes, for their children.

Women had no access to higher professions, which required training and education, though even in the anti-feminine society of Attica a few women succeeded in becoming educated; but these were exceptions like Cimon's sister Elpinice, or Aspasia, later Pericles' mistress, or Diotima, Socrates' friend. It was only the *hetaerae*, of whom we shall speak elsewhere, who could ignore the tabus of society because they did not apply to them.

Normally women in Athens had no legal rights at all. Never in all her life did a woman succeed in attaining personal freedom, since the authority of the master of the house not only extended to the entire property of the *oikos*, that is, the family, but included all persons of the household and thus the wife. This *kyrieia* (authority) was first of all wielded by a girl's father, then by her husband and after his death by his sons; it represented jurisdiction over her person and property. Though at home she was allowed to administer the finances, the *thesauros*, she was not legally entitled to do business exceeding a half medimnos (55 pounds) of barley. At the law court her interests were represented by her master or *kyrios* and she was neither accepted as a trustworthy witness, nor alone allowed speak in her own case. But this *kyrieia* was not universal in Greece. Thus women in Boeotia, Thessaly, Delphi, Megara, Amorgos and Tenos had rights of property and the power to conduct litigation. In the legal code of Gortyna, too, a woman was entitled to possess property, to litigate and to take an oath.

If a woman entered into marriage, that is, if her father traded her to a man, she was completely at the latter's mercy, unless some male person could be found who would take sides with her and make a public complaint of "bad treatment" on her behalf. But if she desired to escape from a joyless marriage by entertaining a love-affair, she thereby placed in jeopardy the life of her lover, who, if the pair were caught in the act, could be killed by the husband, as Eratosthenes was by Euphiletus, according to a forensic speech by Lysias. In addition her husband had to repudiate her, for the law said:

"If a man catches anyone in the act of adultery, he who has caught him (i.e. the husband), is not allowed to live longer with his wife in the married state. If however he does this, he is to be deprived of his honour and his civil rights; further a woman, with whom a lover has been caught, is not allowed to attend divine service. If she nevertheless enters the temple, she exposes herself to every kind of assault, short of death, without retribution."

(Demosthenes, Speech against Neaera)

The divorce-court also applied unequal criteria to husbands and wives. The man was allowed simply to "repudiate" his wife, in which case however he had to give back her dowry, or if he could not, he had to pay a high rate of interest on it. The woman on the other hand could not in any way dissolve her marriage without masculine support. She required the support of her relatives, either father or brothers, who automatically became her *kyrioi* on the dismissal of the husband. She had to appear personally before the competent magistrate and submit a written petition for divorce in order legally to risk "leaving" her husband. Even when the man was adjudged responsible for the breakdown of the marriage, the children always remained with the father. After a divorce had become absolute, the woman was allowed to marry again.

Compensation for the woman is found in the statute book of the Dorian town of Gortyn, where the guilty husband had to pay his wife an indemnity.

The Greek legal institution that was the most degrading for women was the law of the inherited daughter. When an Athenian died without leaving any sons his grandsons would have had a legal title to inherit above his daughters. To obviate this the mother as daughter of the testator became the "inherited daughter", i.e. she became as it were an appendage of the inheritance and her nearest male relative, mostly her uncle or her cousin, had the right to acquire and marry her and receive the inheritance if she was not ready to forgo it without compensation. If the inherited daughter was already married, she had to dissolve her marriage and fulfil her duty to her kinsfolk. It was only in Gortynian law that she was allowed to avoid marriage with the relative who was entitled to marry and inherit her, and that by means of a division of the inheritance. Moreover, as opposed to Athens, in the Dorian towns women had legal rights, though these were limited. An inherited daughter, it is true, had certain advantages; thus for example if she were poor she could claim a dowry from her kinsfolk, and she had to be treated well by her husband; but all this

24

mattered little compared with the monstrous invasion of the woman's personal life.

To sum up, the social and legal position of women in Attica was not exactly calculated to produce important female personalities. Nevertheless the feminine element played an important part in all the arts. Less as an active part, simply as an object about which to think, write or scoff, and one that could be portrayed. Women—always, however, as an inseparable part of man's world—were involved in the great process of development of the Greek drama, and the humanization of philosophy and poetry extended to the partner who had no legal rights but who began to be seen as a fellow human being.

We have no space here for analysis of the female characters the tragedians present to us. Neither the demonic Clytemnestra in Aeschylus, nor the embittered, vindictive Electra nor her sister Iphigenia, who has to sacrifice her life, are conceived as mythical characters, far removed from reality. All of them not only served as vehicles for the ideas behind the drama, they must also be seen as the poet saw them—real human beings who happened to be women. How could one grant an Alcestis the moral victory over her husband or Antigone's courage, self-sacrifice and greater insight into justice than King Creon if one believed in the inferiority of woman? It is a strange contradiction that the Athenians allowed themselves to be taught standards of moral conduct by an Antigone, while they shut their womenfolk up in the *gynaeconitis*.

Many are the conjectures that have been made about Euripides and his attitude toward the female sex and the most varied answers have resulted. Some regard him as the enemy of women that Aristophanes made him into in his 'Thesmophoriazusae,' others like U. v. Wilamowitz, have described him as

"the man who discovered woman and the moral conflicts that arise from the relations between the sexes, for poetry" (*see* I. Bruns, Frauenemanzipation in Athen 4).

Like his predecessors Euripides was not concerned with winning social recognition for women by way of larger social rights.

This theme was to be reserved for the comedian, the eminently political and politically conservative Aristophanes. Euripides had shone a light into the soul of woman and found the purpose of her life in love. He must be given the credit of having looked into the innermost recesses of his heroines' hearts and thus removing such terrible crimes as Medeas' murders or Phaedra's passions from the incomprehensibility of god-given fate and placing them in the field of human experience and judgement.

Three famous women-dramas by Aristophanes have come down to us: "Lysistrata", "Thesmophoriazusae" (Women at the Thesmophoria) and "Ecclesiazusae" (Women in Parliament). From the problems thrown open by these plays it is possible to estimate accurately to what extent the situation of women had grown into a real problem at the end of the fifth century as a result of the collapse of the Attic empire and the fiasco of the Peloponnesian war, but also in view of the unprejudiced discussion of social problems by the Sophists. Historians have spoken about the emancipation of women started by a circle of educated women, perhaps led by Aspasia. At all events Aristophanes' women-dramas can not be explained by the diverting paradox of women as clever operators. Apart from numerous glimpses of everyday life and comic situation they make a fresh judgement of women. There is Lysistrata concluding peace, intelligent and statesmanlike, and Praxagora taking upon herself the role of female demagogue in order to win social equality. That in practice everything remains caught up in farce and obscenity, is not so much due to the inadequacy of the ideas or of the female leaders but to the inadequacy of human beings, who ought to be living in a paradise of complete equality.

Aristophanes brought onto the stage what Plato expressed in his principal works. In his 'Republic' he draws up a model of a community without family and marriage. The woman is made the equal of the man in rights and duties and enjoys equal opportunities of training and education.

His great successor Aristotle, however, takes a step backward by taking greater account of reality. He sticks to the existing form of marriage but is concerned with giving it a deeper purpose by according the wife a partnership in the household, even though in natural gifts she cannot match her husband:

"People do not only live together for the sake of procreating children but also for the sake of the things that concern life. Tasks are apportioned right at the beginning; they are different for husband and wife; in this way they help one another and complement one another with their different capacities."

(*Nicomachaean Ethics 9, 14*)

Despite the endeavours of the philosophers there was no essential change. At the time of Demetrius of Phalerum, female vigilantes were introduced into Athens, whose duty it was to keep an eye on decency, morals and a seemly modesty especially in clothing. It was not until Hellenistic times that the lot of women changed, though more de facto than de jure; the gates of freedom were pushed ajar now and again.

So far we have spoken of the free woman, the citizen's wife or daughter, who, despite the limitations imposed upon her, was regarded as a full member of the community. But about one fourth of the population in classical times were slaves, who existed at all levels, but mostly at the lower, of life in the ancient world. Allowed a restricted right to marry and have children, but always at the complete mercy of their masters despite minimal legal protection, they worked in almost all branches of handicraft and commerce, in the house, in agriculture and in the mines. Slave labour was the basis of ancient society, but those with full rights of citizenship wasted little thought and few words on this, the lowest social stratum, so that detailed accounts of the lot of individual slaves are rare. The female slave stood in the shadow of the free woman, when she did not belong to an employer as brothel inmate or female worker. Her most frequent place of work was in the household. Here she could occupy a respected place, work at the side of her mistress and even rise to be her confidante. She was given all the rough work. Euripides makes the unhappy daughter of Priam, Polyxena, outline the picture of a slave's lot, which she as prisoner of war might have expected, were she not doomed to a sacrificial death:

"For well may I find a master hard of heart,
Whoever with his wealth be purchaser
Of me, sister of Hector and his brothers.
Corn in his house he well may force me to grind,
Or sweep the floor, or at the shuttle stand,
Leading a bitter life of enforced days.
Me in the marriage bed some slave will taint,
Bought heaven knows where, though I was fit for princes.
Not now!"

George Allen   (Hecabe, 359—366)

Homer (Il. 23, 705) gives the barter-price for a female slave as four head of cattle and in classical times a slave cost 150—200 drachmae on the average.

The female slave appears in literature and the plastic arts as wet-nurse, nursemaid, maidservant. Euripides' Phaedra makes her nurse, who speaks with astonishing worldly wisdom, into her only confidante, and the nurse in her devotion to the unhappy queen, attempts to enter into the world of feelings and thought of the noble heroes and appeals to her to act in a way that is common sense and practical, even though inglorious, but by a tragic twist her intentions become the occasion of Phaedra's death.

"Phaedra: Awful, the things you say. Be still and let me
Hear no disgusting words like that again!
Nurse: Disgusting, aya, but better for you than fine!
The deed that rescues you stands higher than
The glory you're so proud of—it will kill you!"
                    (Hippolytus, 498—502)

It is not only the female protegés who win and keep the devotion of their nurse. Even the husky Heracles is accompanied on his fateful way to school by a toothless crone.

MARRIAGE AND MARRIED LIFE

The most important step in the life of a Greek woman was marriage. She took this step very young, mostly between 12 and 15. She had spent her childhood in the house of her parents playing ball and hoop, with dolls and spinning tops and on a swing. She had also been initiated into the secrets of domestic economy and weaving and had practised the most important rules of conduct for her coming life, namely humility and silence, since "silence is the adornment of women." (Aristotle, Politics, 1, 13).

She was still practically a child when the decisive event in her life approached. Obtaining a suitable partner was no concern of hers but of her kyrios, usually her father. Frequently the man chosen was a great deal older than she was, since Attic men enjoyed their freedom as long as possible seeing that "marrying, to tell the truth, is an evil, but a necessary evil" (Menander).

If a candidate of equal social rank had been found, possibly with the aid of a female marriage-broker, the bride's father concluded the marriage contract (engyesis) with the future husband and this included negotiations for the girl's dowry consisting mostly of jewelry, clothes and female slaves or of 30 minae as in the case of Neaera's daughter.

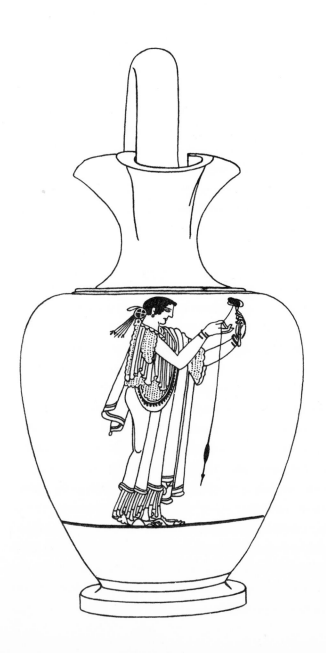

Girl in rich dress spinning

This contract was the sole legal basis for the marriage and might only be concluded if both partners were marriageable; that is, in addition to being of the prescribed age both had to be in possession of full civil rights in order to beget legitimate children. If this condition was not observed, heavy penalties were imposed in Athens—one only needs to remember the famous case brought against the *hetaera*, Neaera, as described by Demosthenes.

After a considerable interval the bride was ceremoniously handed over *(ekdosis)* and matrimony was begun. The wedding celebration was a great family festival. An especially lucky day was chosen for it, most marriages taking place in winter in the marriage month of *Gamelion*. The father and the bride brought sacrifices to the gods. She burnt her children's toys, sometimes also some strands of hair, and thereby took leave of her childhood.

Before the wedding day the bride-bath took place, in Athens in the spring of Kallirrhoe and in other cities in holy rivers or springs. For this purpose a *lutrophoros* was used, a tall vessel with two handles. If anyone died unmarried, this vessel was set up on the grave in order to grant this holy and important ceremony to the dead.

On the morning of the wedding the bride was ceremoniously washed and clothed, and she donned the bridal wreath and veil. Many friends and acquaintances gathered for the wedding feast. Certain comestibles such as bread rolls with sesame seeds were eaten as symbols of fertility. At evening the newly-weds were conducted into their new home. On a cart drawn by oxen or mules the bride sat between her new husband and a bridal companion, whom the husband had to provide. The mule accompanied the team and behind him the wedding-guests joined in the procession led by the bride's mother, all with torches in their hands. The procession sang songs of praise but also rudely humorous ones to the bride and bridegroom and the girls struck up a wedding song. In the groom's house his mother received the young wife, who in performance of her first act in her new home ate a quince, which was supposed to promote fertility, before being conducted by her mother-in-law to the nuptial chamber, which the bridegroom then bolted shut. A sentry was posted outside the door to stop all noise, fun-making, singing and rattling the door. The guests celebrated till the small hours. In the morning the newly-wedded wife welcomed her relations and received presents from them.

HOUSEHOLD DUTIES

Then however, began the serious business of living. The bride was confronted with a complicated household. The servants were subject to her orders, she had to manage the money, arrange the preparation of meals and take over the processing of wool and the making of clothes, or alternatively instruct the female servants in these tasks.

Not every woman would have had such a friendly teacher for a husband as the young wife of Isomachus, who in conversation with Socrates explains vividly the state of his wife when she came to him and what state he trained her to. Xenophon makes him recount: "How was I able to make her so sensible ... when she was not even 15 years old when she came into my house and had lived in very great restriction, seeing, hearing and experiencing very little? Do you not think that I would have had to be satisfied if she was even handy enough to take up wool and make clothes and could see to it that her serving-girls did their routine work? As far as eating and drinking go, she was excellently instructed when she came to me and that seems to me to be really the main thing in the education of both girls and boys." *(Econ. 7)*

A wife's prime duty was to bear children. How often this turned out to be the end of a young wife is shown in many epitaphs:

"Damainatus' excellent daughter Cratista, the dear wife of Archemachus, was received into this dust. Fate put an end to her life as she lay groaning in labour and left a motherless child behind in the house for the husband."

(W. Peek, Greek Epitaphs, Berlin 1960, 83)

Isomachus puts the subject of bringing up children at the beginning of his admonitions. "If the Gods give us children we should consult with one another how to give them the best education. For they are a treasure to both of us and must be our supporters and best guardians in our old age."

Further responsibilities follow:

"It is your duty to remain at home and send out the slaves whose tasks lie outside the house. You must keep an eye on those who work at home, and check what is brought in from outside. You must share out the money to be spent on everything and pay strict attention to what should remain over, making sure you do not spend in one month as much money as is planned for a year. If the wool is brought into the house to you you must take care that they are clothed who need to be, and you must make sure that the dry grain is properly prepared for eating ... One, however, of your responsibilities may not be particularly pleasant for you, namely that when anyone in the house is sick, you must see to it that they are nursed back to health."

We can add that if the wife's ministrations failed, it was her job to concern herself with the laying-out of the corpse and the mourning ceremonies.

Supervision of the messengers, instruction in wool-working, praise and blame, in short the whole direction

28

of servants and slaves lay in her hands. The basic principle of every household was order and good utilization of the rooms since it was only in well-equipped, well-maintained living quarters that comfort could be assured:

"The inmost room requires the most expensive covers and household utensils, the grain must be kept in the driest part of the house, the wine in the cooler part and then where there is plenty of light, the household utensils and workers, who need plenty of light. I (Isomachus) also showed her the rooms for the people to live in, which are so equipped that they are cool in summer and warm in winter."   *(Xen., Econ.9)*

Now the reader is presented with the good order in the chests of the ideal housewife:

"We started by putting together the things we use for sacrifices. Then we set the female wardrobe for holidays apart, then the man's holiday clothes and military uniform, the bedclothes for the women's room and those for the men's, women's shoes and men's shoes, each in a separate place. The weapons had their own special place, as did the various utensils for wool-spinning, the grinding of corn, the preparation of vegetables, washing, baking and eating, and from everything we selected things for our daily use and things for festive occasions."

Isomachus promises his dear young wife a magnificent reward if she shows so much industry and house-wifely virtue:

"The nicest thing of all is this: if you succeed in appearing better than I am and making me myself your servant you need never fear that with advancing years you will enjoy less honour in the house; on the contrary you can be sure that the older you get and the more you are a good helpmate for me and an even better protectress for the children of the house, the more you will be respected and honoured in the house."

Not a few Attic women trod this path to its end and in death were honoured by their husbands with epitaphs, which described their lives with significant brevity:

"Neither clothes nor gold did this woman admire in life, no, she loved only her husband and industry. Now your husband Antiphitos adorns your grave instead of your blooming beauty, Dionysia, and your youth."

(Peek 92)

The lives of poor women, just those who had no male protection, seldom became the subject of literary or philosophical interest. Here too it is the lapidary résumé—hewn into stone that give us informations, it is as if they were intended to pay a debt to the dead woman, for whom life in all its pitilessness was to blame. Here we read:

"... a hard-working and thrifty woman was I, Nikarete, and now lie here in my grave"   *(Peek 103)* or

"Lying on the rocky seashore to leeward I, diligent Isias, see many a ship sailing along. But I lie here dead on a lonely shore and have left behind two children and a husband. When I was alive, I earned my family's greatest esteem by my work. Welcome! Divine Providence grant that my family remain ever unharmed, also for my piety's sake" *(Peek 128)*

and the following inscription reveals completely an unhappy life:

"Passer-by, look upon this tomb here and shed a tear
for the unhappy woman, who washed up by the waters
of the sea far from home lies buried in the depths
of the earth. Aline, at home somewhere in
Phoenicia,
all alone, driven hither and thither, a poor woman of
the people: this is how I, Apas, call to you: for pity's
sake turn your steps hither and shed a tear:
and thank the one who generously buried her here."
(Peek 235)

RELIGION AND CULT

"Barely seven years of age
I walked in the procession,
Ten years old, a miller girl
Of goddess Artemis,
Then in a little saffron dress I played the bear at
Brauron,
Then as a lovely virgin I carried the festal basket
And the string of dried figs."

(Aristophanes, Lysistrata 640—647)

This is how the chorus of women in Aristophanes' 'Lysistrata' enumerates the roles a girl could play in the public ritual festivals. From their earliest years children were involved in religious life: this was the best way to learn about the multifarious festivals and customs. If women were not accorded a place in political life an exception was made in the case of the civic cults. Women took part in almost all religious celebrations. In the cult they found a sphere in which they could satisfy their desire for collective action and ceremonial participation in public life.

Some of them became priestesses and as such occupied a highly respected position. Here is an inscription from the tomb of a priestess from Miletus:

"The signpost of this town gives your greetings to the
holy priestess. Such honour befits a diligent woman.
She led you into the mountains and carried all
the sacraments and holy vessels whenever she
stepped forward in the procession before the
whole city. Her name, if a stranger asks it:

Alcmaeonis, daughter of Rhodius. She knew her
part of all good things." *(Peek 178)*.

Chamyne, the priestess of Demeter, was the only woman allowed to be present at the games in the stadium at Olympia, the priestess of Hera in Argos gave her name to the year, and the priestess of Athena appeared in public with all the attributes of the goddess. In Athens, Polias, the priestess of Athena, received the gifts of newly-wedded couples on the Acropolis and, pomegranate in hand, promised the young wife fecundity, or she received the contributions that fell to the goddess at birth and death. Subordinate to her were the virgins of aristocratic birth, who lived for a time on the citadel and whose office as *Arrephori* it was to carry holy objects in baskets through an underground passage in the course of the magic fertility rites.

The Panathenaean festivals, also in honour of Athena, were held annually in June and July and every four years were celebrated with especial pomp. On the eve of the great procession, which we can see on the *Cella* frieze of the *Parthenon*, the youth of the city danced on the citadel. The climax of this procession of the citizenry was the presentation of a large square robe, the *peplos*, to Athena Polias. The noblest virgins and women had the honour of weaving this robe. It took them nine months and was handed over to the priest and priestess by a young girl of noble birth. As *Canephori*, young girls from the foremost families carried the holy sacrificial vessels to the scene of the festival.

The greatest and perhaps most widespread women's festival in all Greece, which was celebrated without men, was the *Thesmophoria*, dedicated to Demeter and Kore. It was celebrated in spring at sowing time and lasted three days. During this time married women with full citizen rights withdrew, lived in leafy shelters in the sanctuary and devoted themselves to strange rites. Closely linked with the *Thesmophoria* was the *Skiri*, celebrated in May and June. The women threw living piglets, pine branches and loaves in the shape of snakes and phalli down into underground caves called *megara* to the Earth goddesses below. Then at the *Thesmophoria* it was the task of specially favoured "retrieving women" to fetch up the rotting remains to the surface, to mince them, lay them upon the altar and then mix them with the cornseed. In this way the fertility of the soil was ensured for the coming harvest. The third day of the

Thesmophoria was called *Kalligeneia*—beautiful offspring. The women implored fertility and beauty for their children as for the fields.

The spring festival of *Anthesteria* (January/February) was the time of the Basilinna, the wife of the archon Basileus. Together with fourteen other women, she was allowed to perform secret rites in a sanctuary of Dionysus opened only once a year and to celebrate holy marriage with the resurrected god. It was here that the young Phrano, daughter of the Hetaera Neaera, fell foul of the law because without possessing the full citizen rights of an Attic woman, she performed the holiest of rites, thereby blaspheming the gods and despising the laws. The ecstatic religions were the particular domain of women throughout the whole of antiquity. Even the Athens of Aristophanes echoed with the Adonis-howls of the Attic women, who shrieked from the rooftops in mourning for the dead sweetheart of Aphrodite. More dangerous, not only for the participants, was the time when the female followers of Dionysus gave themselves up to an orgiastic frenzy and clad as Maenads in an animal's skin and holding the thyrsos-staff in their hands, ranged through the woods of Parnassus awaiting the god and taking him in with the meat of animals they had torn to pieces in their madness. The Maenads' frenzy and the god's riotous followers were a favourite subject of myth and of the plastic arts. Whether the orgiastic procession and the alcoholic frenzy could generally be kept within bounds at orderly festivals such as the urban and rural *Dionysia* or the *Lenaea* at Athens, need not concern us here. But as late as the time of Pausanias (second century A.D.) Attic and Delphian women, the *Thyiades*, gathered every second winter on Parnassus to pay homage to Dionysus in orgiastic celebrations.

At home the woman supervised the giving of gifts to the gods on particularly festive occasions such as births, marriages and deaths. In the cult of the dead she had to see that graves were tended and take care of the appointed gifts which meant so much in retaining the favour of the departed spirits.

CLASSICAL PERIOD: SPARTAN LIFE

"Ah, dearest Lampito, welcome here from Sparta!
Oh, what a radiant beauty's yours, sweet friend!
How fresh your face, how vigorous your body!
You'd strangle a steer!"   (*Lysistrata, 77—81*)

This is how the elegant Athenian, Myrrhine, satirizes the rough, peasant appearance of her Spartan sister. In this way she, or rather Aristophanes, not only points to the very different ideals of beauty in Athens and Sparta but also to the very different way of life of the Spartan woman. The latter did not belong to the tender sex—she was raised in a body-steeling discipline and was not confined within the limits of the women's quarters, hostile to mind and body alike.

Like the boys, the girls were trained in physical education. Naked, they practised running and wrestling, threw the javelin and the discus, took part in competitions, learned singing, dancing and the mastery of musical instruments. As Plutarch reports, the unclothed girls gathered for processions in the presence of the lads. They sang and danced, but they also possessed the famous Spartan quickwittedness and a sharp tongue. They were used to judging their masculine opposite numbers, to dealing out praise and blame and to occupying themselves also with the political decisions of the men. It is quite easy to believe Plutarch when he describes the completely unerotic character of these occasions, for where would nudity be most easily forgotten if not in a community of naked people? The fashion, too, of the Spartan woman's robe, open at the side, was felt as immoral and criticized only by foreigners.

This emancipation and the body-steeling training of girls had its cause in the very conditions of existence among the Lacedemonians. They lived as a minority in their own state, in constant fear of the subjugated aboriginals, who worked as helots on their estates and were ever ready to revolt. The number of full-blooded Spartans declined rapidly during centuries so that in classical times only a few hundred were left. It was this paramount defence requirement within the state that resulted in the upbringing of men being centred upon toughness and preparedness for battle, but the same was true of the women, who had above all to be the healthy, strong mothers of sons and who, moreover, during the frequent absences of their menfolk on military service, had to play the respected and feared *despoina* (mistress) in the management and administration of the estate.

This situation also determined Sparta's moral norms. A much freer relationship prevailed between the sexes. To secure the existence of the state it was necessary to use practices which are unimaginable in the case of other Greek states. The ageing husband himself looked for a young lover for his wife and recognized their children as his own. Even the sharing of partners married to others was not offensive so long as it produced children. In general, however, the young wife did not see much of her husband, who only visited her secretly at night, to leave her again soon and sleep with his comrades in separate apartments.

This "secret" marriage was begun with the rape of the bride, a relic of a former age, which had remained alive in Sparta. Marriage served to produce children—that was its chief purpose. Parents had to have their children inspected by some public authority and to expose them if they had physical defects or looked puny. From the age of six onwards the state took the education of children out of their mothers' hands, so that no close emotional ties could develop.

Sparta's mothers, simple and patriotic, did not expect love from their sons, but courage. The epigraph, "Rather upon it than without it," referring to the warrior's shield, indicates the mentality of the Spartan "mother of heroes." Aristotle deplored the Spartan matriarchy but the women of Sparta had their answer pat. It is said of Gorgo, the wife of Leonidas, that when someone said

"You Lacedemonian women are the only ones who lord it over your menfolk",

she replied,

"Yes, but then we are the only ones who still bring men into the world."

(Plutarch, Lycurgus 14).

THE HELLENISTIC PERIOD: A COSMOPOLITAN AGE

In the 4th century a new power had entered world-history—Macedonia. Far away in Northern Greece, hardly touched by culture and civilization, it was destined to be the springboard for a thorough-going transformation of the ancient world. While the Greek *poleis* were ruining one another with petty wars and their governments contending with civil strife, Philip II vigorously took possession of the Macedonian crown and secured his dynasty, and building up an army of singular striking power, made himself master of Greece. Athens and her allies were defeated by him at Chaeronea in 338 B.C., and the way was clear for a "panhellenic punitive war" against Persia. Alexander, his famous son, trod this path —his victorious armies reaching as far as the Indian Ocean—and at his early death in 323 B.C. he had conquered an empire which in its diversity and gigantic extent was no less difficult to govern than to administer. Greece, Persia, Syria, Phoenicia and Egypt had been occupied by his armies. But in order even to strengthen this enormous empire the deep gulfs that had separated the peoples living at completely different levels of culture gradually had to be overcome. Alexander worked upon this problem, applying his fusion policy, demonstrated symbolically in 327 B.C. at the great wedding in Susa, at which he married Roxane, the daughter of an Iranian prince and 80 of his generals married Iranian women. When Alexander died, he had no successor to continue his work, and the inevitable result was a partition of the empire. In long struggles against one another his most powerful commanders divided his empire among themselves in the form of independent monarchies with the result that by the end of the 4th century three great powers confronted one another: the Ptolemaic empire in Egypt, the Seleucid empire in Western Asia with Syria as its centre, and the Antagonid empire consisting of Macedonia and Greece. After 280 B.C., a fourth power, the Attalid empire, emerged at Pergamum.

None of Alexander's successors (the *Diadochi*) continued his fusion policy but the fertilizing and levelling process that pervaded all areas of culture and society was not to be halted. It was above all Greek culture that spread throughout Asia and fused with the oriental heritage. Greek became the "*koine*" or lingua franca of the whole region; Greek art, philosophy and science retained their hegemony even at the royal courts of Macedonia and the Orient. This involved fundamental changes that affected all spheres of life. Additionally there was an

34

enormous increase in trade, which led to the extension of banking and monetary circulation, to centres of production arising in the great cities and to the emigration of the pauperized town and country population into new areas of the empire, with the resulting disruption of family close ties. The increase in cross-natural contacts stimulated the development of the sciences and especially of the technical applied sciences, brought about the re-assessment of many moral and ethical values in the new schools of philosophy and encouraged a greater variety in the forms of art. The three hundred years from Alexander to the Battle of Actium in 31 B.C., which encompassed the most varied political, social and cultural phenomena, are much more difficult to survey than, say, the classical 5th century centred as it was in Athens. The Greek ferment, however, united these three centuries into a historic epoch, though the demarcation implied by "Hellenism" as proposed by J. G. Droysen in 1836 is not really precise enough either chronologically or in respect to content, and no attempt will be made to insist upon it here.

Hellenism—means world empire, world cities and world culture. These rapidly progressing transformations could not remain without effect upon the private lives of men. The Greek cities of the mother country had lost their political independence. The public interest was no longer to be managed by the sovereignty of arms-bearing citizens in their popular assemblies. People were subjected completely to the policies of the Macedonian masters, paid homage to them and slowly changed from citizens of city-states to citizens of countries. Hellenistic man was fashioned by home and family, by a respectable life in quiet seclusion, even contemplation, far removed from political activity.

In philosophy, both among Stoics and Epicureans, private life became the centre of attention. Happiness was to be found in seclusion; exclusiveness and political passivity became the ideal of life. For the woman this re-assessment of the content of life of course represented a gain. She became mistress in the home and thus the ground for her emancipation was prepared.

In the mother country, Greece, it is true, the out-of-date legal sanctions were largely upheld and no political rights were bestowed, but the woman in the territories of Alexander's successors (the *Diadochi*), especially in Egypt, possessed a considerable measure of independence. In Egyptian eyes she was entitled to conduct litigation and business and only needed her *kyrios* as supporter and witness to her identity for agreements concluded in the Greek language. But in Greece, too, the general process of individualization did not stop short of women. The woman, it is true, continued to remain at home, but in a home transformed by the new luxury, one in which she possessed her own apartment, saloons, courtyards, etc. Formerly love of display had been lavished almost exclusively on public buildings and temples; during the Hellenistic period the private home, too, attracted the work of architects, painters and sculptors. The palaces of the princes provided models which the rich citizens only too gladly copied.

Libraries and guest-rooms were an essential part of the prosperous Hellenistic private residence. The interior decoration was both luxurious and artistic. Frescoes, stuccowork and sculptures, costly furniture, cushions and covers created an atmosphere of comfort and wealth.

The lady living in these cultivated surroundings was as a rule no longer the uneducated woman of the classical era. Perhaps as a girl she had gone to school, had a knowledge of literature and was able, if she was adventurous enough, to become a student of the philosophers and conquer the world of the spirit formerly reserved to men. It is no accident that among the philosophers and artists of the Hellenistic period are to be found the names of women. The Epicureans accepted female members in their community; Epicurus himself corresponded with the daughter of Metrodorus, and the Stoics were by no means mysogynist.

But it was above all the demonstrably numerous female disciples of Pythagoras who set new moral standards for marriage and family life. They understood marriage as an equal partnership of man and woman and demanded chastity and marital fidelity both of husband and wife. The transformation of life into a private affair favoured the emotional rapprochement between partners in marriage and love-marriages ceased to be unusual. The Stoic Antipater of Tarsus (2nd century B.C.) recommends that the choice of a wife should depend less on riches, parentage and beauty and more on the mentality and morality of the family, and the educational principles by which the girl had been raised, if the husband wanted his marital ideals to be fulfilled, since

"other friendships and love affairs are like hybrids which arise from two things being joined, like beans or the like. The union of man and woman, on the other hand, is like a harmonious mixture, such as wine and water."

In art, everyday happenings become subjects worthly of representation. The poetess, Anyte of Tegea (c. 300 B.C.) ploughs virgin soil with her artistic epigrams on animals.

To a goat she writes:

"Red reins, O Goat, these boys have set about
Thy neck, a muzzle on thy shaggy snout,
And round God's temple ply their mimic race,
That he may look on them with kindly face."

W. H. D. Rouse

Nossis of Locri (c. 300 B.C.) wrote cult poems to Aphrodite but also epigrams affectionately portraying the world of children. Despite life in large cities and the "enlightenment wave" which widened the Greek woman's horizon, the feminine tendency towards religiosity persisted uninterrupted, although the Olympian gods were now scarcely regarded as powers capable of determining fate. The goddesses on Olympus are stripped of their majesty and portrayed like the beauties of the earth to the delight of lascivious eyes. A slipper is pushed into Aphrodite's hand to enable her to repulse or to allure the eager Pan according to the likes or dislikes of the artistically-minded observer. In their amorous anguish the girls now call out:

"... Shine brightly, Moon,
  this murmured spell is for you and Hekate
  dark of the earth, who scares the trembling whelps,
  visiting the barrowed dead where blood rots blackly.
  Hail, dreadful one, be with me till I've made
  this magic fiercer than any made by Circé, ..."

J. Lindsay   (Theocritus, Simaetha 12—14)

Theocritus' witch winds the bird-wheel round, throws flour into the flame, melts the wax-image of her lover, burns laurel leaves and reeks with bran in Selene's mild light. People believe in astrologers and magicians from the East, soothsaying and oracle-interpretation thrive as never before and the redeemer-religions spread widely. Besides the Eleusinian mysteries, those of Andamia in the Peloponnese especially attract a large number of adherents. Women, girls and even female slaves were to be found among the initiates. To put a curb on feminine extravagence in dress and give the impression of a certain equality, dress regulations were issued for believers:

"Those who celebrate the mysteries have to go barefoot and wear a white gown, the women wearing clothes which are not translucent and do not possess hems of more than an inch. The women in the throng must wear an undergarment and a dress of linen worth not more than 100 drachmae while the girls must have a linen or cotton undergarment and a dress worth not more than 1 mina. The slave girls must have a linen or cotton undergarment and a dress worth not more than 50 drachmae. Of the holy women (who have a share in the leadership) the married ones must wear a linen or other undergarment, non-iridescent, and a dress worth not more than 2 minae, the unmarried girls a linen undergarment and dress worth not more than 100 drachmae ... None may wear gold ornaments or red or white make-up or a hair-ribbon or a sophisticated hair-style or sandals, apart from those made of felt or of leather from animal sacrifices ... If a woman dresses otherwise as prescribed or wears anything else that is forbidden, the women's superviser must not allow this and has the right to censure her: the forbidden object must then be dedicated to the gods."   (J. Leipoldt, Die Frauen der Antike und im Urchristentum, 49 foll.)

The cult of Adonis is wide-spread. In Theocritus' "Women at the Festival of Adonis" we learn of the crowds in the streets of Syracuse and the festive mood of two Greek ladies. From Egypt the cult of Isis spread all over the Mediterranean. Isis the mother of God becomes, together with Serapis and Ammon, the leading deity in the Hellenistic world.

Hellenism involved, however, not only social differentiation, the division into educated and uneducated and the dissolution of a citizen-community in which rich and poor shared alike in the cultural heritage of the polis; it meant more than anything else monarchy, with a sovereign ruler over everyone. Divine kingdom and ruler-cult were strange to the Greeks—these were a legacy of the Orient; nevertheless Greece was familiar with the outstanding personality who became a patron of the arts, even though the splendor of tyrants' courts had long passed away. Coming into the limelight of history at the side of these kings, were female personalities whose unscrupulousness and thirst for power enabled them to exercise great influence upon the politics and art of empires. They could neither claim any legal basis for their position nor any precedent in tradition; on the contrary, the idea of women at the head of the state was impossible whether in Greek or Oriental life, the only exception being in Egypt.

In the 4th century the Carian King Mausolus had made his sister Artemisia his wife and bequeathed her the royal power in the event of his death. For the creation of the monumental tomb for her husband, which was subsequently reckoned as one of the seven wonders of the world, this energetic woman had engaged the most celebrated artists in Greece, hoping by this means to raise a monument to herself as well as to her husband.

At the beginning of the series of demonic heroines of Hellenism stands Olympias, daughter of the King of Epirus, wife of Philip II and mother of Alexander the Great. After the king's death she aspired to the royal power in Macedon and did not shrink from intrigue and the murder of relatives. But she was doomed to failure, being stoned to death by the blood-relatives of her victims. Her daughter, Cleopatra, sister by the same parents of Alexander, was more likeable and less blood-thirsty. During her husband's campaigns she carried on the government of the country as Queen of Epirus. The numerous women of the Alexandrine dynasties (the *Diadochi*)—the Berenices, Stratonices, Laodices, Cleopatras and Arsinoes—distinguish themselves by more or less activity in accordance with their natural inclinations, but seldom did any of them die a natural death, or die without committing some crime or other. Even the most celebrated of them surrounded their brilliant rise to power with the corpses of their relatives, whom they had coldbloodedly murdered whenever they looked like potential rivals for husband and throne. In this respect these ladies were apt pupils of their masculine partners.

Arsinoe II, daughter of Ptolemy I and Berenice I, achieved the highest point of her career, after two marriages and two crowns, in her union with her younger brother, Ptolemy II, ruler of Egypt. This marriage of brother and sister of the same parents was contrary to Greek custom, according to which only half-brothers and half-sisters might intermarry, but it accorded fully with Persian tradition and did not offend Egyptian sensibilities. The Greek poets like Theocritus found in the *Hieros Gamos* (holy wedlock) of the divine brother and sister, Zeus and Hera, the justification for and sanctification of this incestuous marriage, which allotted the thirty-eight year old Arsenoe the role of queen-consort at the side of the weak Ptolemy.

Marriages of brother and sister were the rule in the Alexandrine dynasties (the *Diadochi*); even the last of the Ptolemaeans, the sensational Cleopatra VII, was formally wedded to her brother.

In the newly-founded city of Alexandria, one of the greatest centers for research and culture in the ancient world was organized—the Museum *(Museion)*. Its gigantic library was presided over by the learned poet Callimachus. Arsinoe II surrounded herself with a whole circle of scholars and artists; at the Ptolemaic court were brilliant women, to whose beauty and culture the men had to pay a courtly devotion. The demanding queen had poems written in her honour. Theocritus likens her to the most beautiful of all women, Helen, or even to Aphrodite herself. Her husband-brother, Ptolemy, had founded a cult in honour of their common parents as "Saviour Gods"—*Theoi Soteres*—and this was celebrated every four years with artistic and athletic competitions. His wife Arsinoe II Philadelphos—"brother-loving"—was the first woman in the ancient world to be raised to the status of divinity when she died in 270 B.C. at the age of 46. The *Thea Philadelphos*—"brother-loving" goddess—was given her own temple with a priestess and was honoured together with the old-established gods in all Egyptian places of worship. In addition Ptolemy founded for himself and his deceased wife the cult of the brother/sister gods, the *Theoi Adelphoi*, which was combined with the state cult of Alexander. Arsinoe II was raised to the rank of a local deity, cities, buildings and streets being named after her and coins of the realm bore her likeness. Arsinoe II is the prototype of the Hellenistic princess, of the woman who has broken through the barriers of a man's world. Though of course as queen-consort she was an exceptional case, her example did not fail to have its effect upon the Hellenistic woman's attitude to life. One class especially took advantage of the cult of women and beauty at the queen's court: the *hetaerae*.

THE HETAERAE

"One maintains a hetaera not only for pleasure, as a mistress, but also for the daily care and service of one's person. One marries a respectable woman, on the other hand, to beget legitimate children of equal birth and to have a faithful watch-dog in the house." *(Demosthenes, Speech against Neaera).*

The Greeks stuck to monogamy. A man married only one wife and knew what to expect from her: legitimate children and the supervision of the home. Domestic virtue and the absence of flirtation and all excess were the portion of the Greek wife, at least of those who were accepted and respected. But what place was there for joy, for beauty, high-spirits and gratification of the senses? Did the lovely, friendly girls with the translucent garments and ravishing bodies exist only in the imagination of vase-painters? Can the aggressive eroticism of the Maenads and their satyr games be explained by religious devotion and hallowed tradition?

Today it is difficult to understand how obvious and necessary were the naiveté, the unclouded affirmation of corporal sensuality and the enjoyment associated with crude eroticism which made up Greek life and art and have kept them so attractively alive for centuries. We are weighed down by the heavy legacy of Christianity and the "purifying" view of the Greeks represented by classicism. Thus the sunny side of ancient Greek female existence, namely the phenomenon of the hetaerae, moves all too easily into the ambit of modern prostitution, and we are intuitively inclined to transfer to antiquity the compassion and revulsion we feel might be due to the pitiable creatures of the modern world. But this is a grave error.

Ancient marriage was not what its modern counterpart can be, and a woman could only be looked at as a being beloved and desired by the man. Thus the girls who only had their sophisticated femininity to throw onto the scales and knew how to make a work of art out of themselves, had much greater possibilities than the married woman of participating in public life, of following the pursuits of men, of exercising influence over them and penetrating into their intellectual world and thus of putting themselves on an equal footing with them.

One only needs to think of Aspasia, who lived with Pericles but could not enter into any binding union with him because she did not possess Attic civil rights. She came from Miletus and lived in Athens, perhaps as a

Hetaera putting on her sandals

hetaera, but at all events at Pericles' side, not in the traditional way of an Athenian woman, but in the society of philosophers, artists and scholars. She must have had a noteworthy influence on the great statesman. Nevertheless, or perhaps just because of that, she became the target of the comic dramatists, who attempted to get at Pericles with attacks upon Aspasia. Her sagacity was almost a byword in Athens and husbands sent their wives to her for instruction. This woman stood in the forefront of women's emancipation, as it were, and to a small extent built a bridge between the female citizen and the hetaera.

By the fourth century, other famous hetaerae had begun to devote themselves to philosophy and the arts and to produce literary works.

Extra-marital love-relationships were a matter of course for the Greek man. This division into domestic duty and public pleasure was socially accepted even though the situation continually gave rise to conflicts. *Hetaera* means mistress; as a change from the boring respectability of a wife she offered intellect and beauty, a cheerful lack of constraint and sexual pleasures. She had learnt her trade, could play a musical instrument and dance. Some climbed the ladder of love to the highest rungs and became celebrated mistresses, their names inseparably linked with the great men of intellect and politics, and must have had a similar fascination for their times to that which film stars have for ours. In the works of their contemporaries their brilliance comes down to us.

There is Phryne, the beauty, mistress of Praxiteles, who modelled for his Cnidian Aphrodite and spread her fame by means of a gilded statue set up in Delphi. She was of such *hybris* (overweening pride) and her beauty had brought her such riches that she was able to pledge herself to restore the walls of Thebes, destroyed by Alexander. At the festival of Poseidon in Eleusis she revealed the seductive art of strip-tease: before the assembled Greeks she disrobed and went into the sea. It is said that thereupon the painter Apelles painted his Aphrodite Anadyomene. The Athenians were enthusiastic about her physical charms, but also considered her to be atheistic and tried to accuse her of blasphemy. Hyperides, her friend and defence counsel, rescued her by means of a trick unheard of in the annals of Attic justice: he made her open her dress and display her bosom to the judges. How could this beautiful servant of Aphrodite be an atheist? She was acquitted.

The "highly paid" hetaerae secured great wealth and ruled the men to whom they gave their favours. Alexander's mistress, the hetaera Thais, is said to have demanded of him the destruction of the Persian city of Persepolis because she was a patriotic Athenian. Later on she climbed even higher and became the wife of Ptolemy I and thus queen of Egypt. Lamia, the mistress of Demetrius Poliorcetes, dedicated a pleasure palace in Sicyon. In general rich hetaerae tried to secure for themselves a place in history by commissioning architectural and artistic works.

Some even succeeded in being posthumously deified. In Egypt there was the cult of Aphrodite Belestiche, the hetaera of Ptolemy II, cults of Aphrodite Lamia and Aphrodite Leaena were instituted in Athens, and in Thebes the cult of Aphrodite Lamia. The finest tomb in Athens was that of the hetaera Pythionice, built by order of her lover, the rich Harpolus. The society of these hetaerae was so charming that they were able to attain a very costly celebrity. With mercantile acumen they drove their prices up so that the famous names of erstwhile lovers became a business advertisement.

Thus Lais, destined in old age to taste the bitterness of a courtesan's life, is said to have demanded in the bloom of her youth ten thousand drachmae from Demosthenes, but to have received the answer, "That's too dear a price to pay for repentance."

In addition to the small number of highly-paid hetaerae there was the large number of the more modest ones who had to live on the meagre fare of their daily earnings in the cities, especially in the ports, and who only had available the limited incomes of their lovers. Lucian introduces them to us in his "Discussions with Hetaerae," and we learn of them from cases like Neaera's, preserved in the works of Demosthenes; she was able to exchange the destiny of a slave for the free life of a hetaera. Neaera was one of the seven girls whom the freedwoman and wife of the chef, Nicarete, had bought in tender years, had brought up and educated. The girls were given out by this female pander to be her daughters and then hired out to lovers "with all the pangs of a mother." The lovers were able to claim them exclusively for themselves for a certain period by means of a kind of hiring contract. Then the girls shared the lives of their lovers, often lived with them and celebrated sumptuous love-feasts, at which they had to entertain the revellers with flute-playing, dancing and lively talk. If the pander wished to,

she could sell a girl. Nicarete demanded 30 minae for Neaera. Now two men shared possession of her but she was able to persuade her lovers to get together the money to buy her out of slavery. Then together with the Athenian Phrynio she led the extravagant life of a hetaera, moved from orgy to orgy and acquired a certain stock of female slaves, jewellery and clothes.

The pander's trade was an integral part of the hetaera's existence. She bargained efficiently with her customers, shamelessly exploiting their inclinations. Cleareta, the pander in a comedy of Plautus, gives judgement on her class:

"Why then complain of me for doing just
What my profession demands? Have you ever heard
—No book includes it, 'tis in no picture or poem—
That any pander who knows well her trade
Was ever honest with her customers?"

(Assin. 1, 4)

Besides hetaerae in the power of panders, male and female, who invested a fortune in their upbringing and education, which had to be recovered with profit via the girls' bodies, there were free girls, who from social necessity or desire for life and love trod the path of the hetaerae.

Lucian portrays the circumstances which compel an impoverished family to seek a way out of their difficulties by the sacrifice of their daughter:

Crobyle: "But let me tell you what else you have to do and how to handle men. Otherwise we can't see how we are going to live, dear daughter. Don't you know what a miserably hard time we've had of it the last two years since your father (God rest his soul!) died. When he was alive, we had plenty of everything. He was a coppersmith, a big man in the Piraeus. Every mortal man there will swear there'll never be another like him. After his death I first sold his tongs, his anvil and hammer for two minae and we lived for the next seven months on that. Then I wove, carded wool, and spun it and earned my daily bread by the sweat of my brow. This is how I brought you up, my daughter, and waited for what I hoped for.

Corinna: Do you mean the mine?

Crobyle: No. I counted much more on you keeping me when you were as old as you are now, on you being able yourself to live easily in regular wealth and leisure, to go dressed in purple and have servants.

Corinna: Whatever are you saying, mother? How on earth can you imagine that?

Crobyle: Well, by spending your life in the company of young men, drinking with them and get-

40

ting paid for sleeping with them."

Hetaerae had to be particularly careful how they appeared and the mother describes for her daughter a great model of the type.

Crobyle: "Well first of all she dresses suitably, always looks neat and is cheerful and pleasant with everyone, without giggling on every occasion like you usually do; instead she has a sweet, winning smile. She handles men cleverly, adroitly, disappoints no-one who comes to her or sends for her, but doesn't throw herself at them. When she goes out to a dinner for which she has engaged herself, she doesn't get drunk—that looks so ridiculous and men cannot stand women who do it—and she doesn't gorge herself on the food like people who don't know how to behave, she just touches it with her fingertips. She never talks while she's eating and doesn't cram her cheeks full. She doesn't drink in gulps but in little sips with pauses in between.

Corinna: Oh, mum, but what when she is thirsty?

Crobyle: Well, only then, of course. And she doesn't talk more than is necessary, doesn't laugh at the expense of anyone present and only looks at the man who has hired her. That's why she is so popular with her clients. And when she has to sleep with them, she avoids all pertness and offensiveness and has only one aim—to fascinate the man and make him her lover."

Most lovers soon had their mistresses' complete households round their necks and got to know the seamy side of this sort of existence, what with expenses for clothes and luxuries without which no fashionable hetaera could be happy. Some were fleeced right and left, and became the butt of their acquaintances' mockery, since the hetaerae were as it were public property, the subject of gossip, novels and comedies; the names of over forty hetaerae as names for plays have come down to us and jokes about hetaerae circulated freely.

A third group, in a way the real priestesses of love, ought not to be left out of account—the *hierodules* (sacred slaves). These hetaerae directly entered the service of the love-goddess Aphrodite. Being the property of the sanctuaries of the goddess, they gave themselves to strangers for the good of their sanctuary and the honour of Aphrodite.

The greatest *hierodule* institution was the temple of Aphrodite-Melainis in Corinth, where more than a thousand girls carried on this love-trade in the name and sight of Aphrodite, to the great profit of the sanctuary. The girls were particularly close to the goddess, and they were sent forward whenever it was necessary to offer up a prayer, as in the case of the Persian invasion, when the hetaerae prayed for the deliverance of their country. If anyone wanted to secure a favor from the gods, for example, to win an Olympic victory, one pledged to give a statue or offer a sacrifice, but it was also possible to dedicate slave-girls to the service of love. For some such reason a certain Xenophon gave a hundred girls to Aphrodite of Corinth in 464 B.C. and on the occasion of their ceremonial dedication Pindar wrote a celebratory ode:

"Young maidens with the tender welcome, servants of Peitho, in rich Corinth, ye, that ofttimes make the yellow tears of the green incense rise in vapour while your thoughts fly upwards to the mother of love's yearnings, heavenly Aphrodite, to you is it given, oh daughters, to pluck the fruit of revelling youth upon a luxurious couch, free from reproach. Under compulsion everything is beautiful ... O Lady of Cyprus [Aphrodite] Xenophon overjoyed at the fulfilment of his request has brought a hundred-headed herd of roving girls into your sanctuary." *(Fragment 122)*

Whether the hetaerae carried on their trade in a brothel or independently in higher or lower society, Greek society is unthinkable without them. In addition ordinary uneducated girls, mostly domestic servants or slaves, not unusually—as Demosthenes laconically says—shared the beds of their masters to the great comfort of the men and without putting themselves at the mercy of their wives.

FASHION AND BEAUTY

Fashion is a cross between art and necessity, the region where the creative imagination is skin-tight, current tastes are shaped in their finest nuances and views of life are presented for sale in the form of hats, caps, jackets, trousers and dresses. Clothes are the man—but not his personality. There are national and official uniforms, hardly a club fails to have its "ceremonial dress" just as a particular style of dress identifies rebellious youth in the modern world. Fashion can make itself eminently political, as the sansculottes of the French Revolution well knew. But its real purpose should be something different—to enhance the beauty and distinction of the individual. This was the purpose it served in the ancient world, though the dizzy speed of alternation between short and long, to which we are exposed, was still unknown. A few basic models remained for centuries "in fashion." One theme with variations is the attempt to recognize centuries later the fine distinctions in fashion between old-fashioned and modern even though it is perhaps for us impossible in the disputed realm of taste in this field. Women in ancient as in modern times possessed everyday and Sunday clothes, made from cheap or costly materials, and the servant girl dressed more simply than the lady.

The Homeric woman could be as beautiful as Aphrodite, who seduced Anchises not least by her artful toilette.
"When her he saw, Anchises marvelled much
  At her appearance, at her height and robes;
  She wore a dress that shone as bright as fire,
  And she was richly dight with jewelry;
  Her earrings glowed, a precious necklace wound
  Its golden beauty round her neck and flashed
  With gleaming tints, and on her tender breasts
  Shone like the moon, a wonder to behold."

(Hymn to Aphrodite, 84—90)

In general she wore the *peplos*—a square, coloured woollen cloth used both as a bed-covering and as a cloak. It was fastened with long pins or clasps at the shoulders, fell down over the body in wide pleats and could be gathered into the waist by a girdle. For ceremonial occasions there was a garment of similar cut made of fine white linen—the *pharos*. A fine linen veil covered head and back, one end of it being gracefully held in the hand. Caps, ribbons, metal diadems and jewelry such as that described in the hymn to Aphrodite—the gold and amber chains, the many armbands, ear-rings and expensive clasps—were to be found in the wardrobe and jewel box of the Homeric woman.

Aphrodite and Pan at dice

42

The early archaic period stuck to the heavy woollen peplos with its coloured braiding, lively hues and patterns. This early peplos was longer and very full, so that it had a folded-back flap, the ends or corners of which hung decoratively on either side. In the 6th century the *chiton*, a loose gown made of thin linen, came into fashion in Ionia. With the chiton, a woollen veil-like cloth was worn draped over the head, shoulders, and chest and covering the arms; it ended in two points at the sides.

In late archaic times the sophisticated urban culture of Ionia had influenced almost all spheres of life on the Greek mainland and fashion, too, came under the spell of oriental voluptuousness. The peplos gave way to the elegant linen chiton, as "Dorian dress" even at the time of its renaissance remained inferior to the linen dress of Ionia in elegance and dressiness. Unlike the peplos, the chiton was not pinned up but fastened with buttons on shoulders and upper arms, or more rarely sewn together. It was mostly very long and pleated. It was gathered in at the waist by a girdle over which a wide fold of material fell. If it was desired to wear the chiton as a maternity dress, it was possible to wear a wide belt which was covered in the same way by a wide overhang. The fashionable young ladies, who still stand before us as the Acropolis girls, liked to wear a little pert slanting coat over the finely-pleated chiton. It fell slanting down to the hip leaving one shoulder bare. The hem of the long stole was drawn like a frill over a ribbon and fitted exactly over the side-points and zigzag lines of the chiton hem.

The luxury of the late tyrant epoch was not limited to dress alone. Hair-styles, too, were artistic and fashioned with exquisite care. Metal hoops, crown-like diadems and leather and cloth bandeaus with metal decorations held the usually long curled locks together.

At the beginning of the fifth century as a result of social revolutions, late archaic elegance gave place to a simpler and initially plainer form of dress. The woollen peplos won back some adherents even if the chiton was never to be entirely replaced; in fact a gradual approximation of the two garments to one another took place. The *peplos*, worn open at the side and without girdle by the Spartan lady, usually had a folded flap that hung down either to the waist or even over the hips. A girdle was preferred, though we occasionally see the garment hanging down without one. As with the chiton, a fold was drawn over the girdle and hung down parallel with the

edge of the flap or else the long flap was "overgathered" by means of a second girdle. A cloak completed the toilette of the Greek lady. If she did not wear one, she could draw the flap of the chiton or peplos over her head.

The linen *chiton* now much bulkier with its soft buttoned half-sleeves, the turned-back flaps copied from the peplos and a front fold which fell copiously at the sides and allowed the girdle to be seen in the middle, remained the dignified dress for special occasions.

The chiton could also be less bulky and sleeveless and a short version of it served as domestic uniform and hetaera dress, while in art it was favoured by the Amazons and the goddess of the hunt, Artemis. Chiton and peplos did not only approximate to one another in the way of make-up but they could also be worn together as undergarment and top-dress. The large cloak, or *himation*, was worn by both women and men and left room for creative draping. Usually it was laid over the shoulder, the broad width then being passed over head and thorax, or it could be loosely wound over the hips.

The hairstyles of classical times show an unvarying simplicity. The hair combed and parted above the brow was usually gathered at the back of the head and twisted with ribbons into a high top-knot or it fell in loose plaits over the shoulders. Hairpins were unknown in the ancient world, their function being supplied by cloths and ribbons to keep the hair close to the head. Hairpieces and built-up curls such as were the pride of the Roman lady, were unknown in classical times.

The Hellenistic world was well acquainted with fine textiles: linens from Egypt, silks from China, cottons from India, goldthreaded, expensive, heavy materials and the gossamer silk of Cos. The chiton, the key garment of the Hellenistic period, was now girdled under the bust and left the arms and shoulders bare. The material around the neck was gathered in by a ribbon, while the hem could now be quite wide. The peplos was replaced by a dress without a flap, held up by clasps and worn over the chiton.

Praxinoe, upon whom Theocritus eavesdrops, dresses for the festival of Adonis in the Hellenistic mode:

"Gorgo. Praxinoe, the full gathering of that dress
    does suit you well. Please tell me the stuff's cost.
Praxinoe. O, don't remind me—I'd to pay for it
    more than eight pounds in silver. I assure you,
    I put my soul in every single stitch.
Gorgo. Well, I must say, you couldn't wish for better.

Praxinoe. How sweet of you to say so.

                            Now my cloak,
come, put it on me—and my hat too—mind!
the stylish angle."

Jack Lindsay   (*Theocritus, Festival of Adonis*).

The cloak was now made preferably of thin veil-like fabrics and draped round the body in folds cunningly devised to hide the lines of the figure so that their translucency brought out the colour-effects of the undergarments.

The women of Tanagra also show us the headgear of the Hellenistic lady: a pointed *tholos*-cap with a wide border. It must however be said that hats were not developed as a line of wear in the ancient world. A simple hood for wear by day and night was made by a few fashion houses, just as footwear was an expensive luxury. At home people went barefoot, only putting on shoes for special occasions. The sandal with its straps in many variations was the basic model for the ancient shoemaker. Women however had in addition luxury shoes in a variety of colours, made of expensive materials, ornamented with gold and precious stones, with or without heels, shoes sometimes worth a fortune, that were status-symbols for their wearers.

Jewelry reached the zenith of extravagance in Hellenistic times. Twisted chains of gold wire or band mostly worn as armlet or anklet, were very popular. Masterpieces of the goldsmith's art and of grain and filigree with precious stones or crystal, hung from the lobes of the ladies' ears, adorned their necks and their extravagant hairstyles. The hair was knotted on top of the head, bound up with ribbons, parted and smoothed down, twisted in plaits around the head or, in the case of little girls, allowed to hang in pigtails over the shoulders.

Colour was an integral part of Greek art. The marble temples had coloured reliefs and the great three-dimensional figures on the pediments shone forth in their colour combinations of red, blue and white. Naturalistic colour effects—eyes of crystal with metallic lashes, copper-red lips and nipples—enhanced the verisimilitude of bronze statues gleaming with a golden-brown tint, and the cold whiteness of marble maidens was softened by the milky veil of a wax covering, against which the brilliantly coloured garments and the blazing metal ornaments stood out in shining contrast. The rich colours of a southern sky, the violet-blue sea and the brightness of the sunlight no doubt inspired the Greeks with their passion for colour. Beauty and perfection in art were never merely questions of proportion and outline but also, and always, of colouring, which could become the decisive factor in lending a work of art the illusion of life.

The Greek woman, it is true, had no need to fear for her liveliness, but she, too, felt the need for beauty, for the accentuation of the endowments of nature, which for the women could be vitally necessary. Female beauty was seldom enough a gift laid by the gods in the cradle of the lucky few; but often it was a product of hair-style and make-up based on self-knowledge and discipline. The make-up was of cream, rouge, powder, black and red pencils and the fragrance of an exquisite perfume. The Greek woman who was "beautiful" went about with a painted face and did not despise the little tricks that obscured her physical imperfections.

"If a woman is small of stature, her shoes are lined with cork, if another is tall, she gets a pair of shoes with thin soles and lowers her head down towards her shoulders as she walks. A third has slim hips—they can be padded out. A fourth is plump, so her body is laced in and pinched tight. If she has eyebrows as red as fire she blackens them with pine soot. A woman with a swarthy skin rubs white lead on it, one with a pale skin uses carmine red. If any part of her body is of outstanding beauty, it is revealed. One has beautiful teeth, so she must laugh on every possible and impossible occasion. And when she has no mind to laugh, she stays quietly at home and takes a myrtle twig between her lips so that she always has a smile on them."

(Athen. XIII 568)

When nothing more could be done with natural hair, a wig was resorted to, as is done by a 45-year old hetaera in a dialogue of Lucian, whose make-up tricks were obviously so perfect that her lover was taken in by her pretence to be only 22 years old until he was undeceived by a rival hetaera.

In addition women put oil on their hair, with the resulting smooth coiffures that are seen in ancient statuary.

Of course the Greek woman knew as well as we do what were the essential conditions for a beautiful skin: daily careful cleaning of the whole body. She washed herself at the well in the courtyard, in bowls in the house; the prosperous citizen possessed a bathroom and where one was not available visited the public baths or *balaneia*. There were separate sections for women but we have evidence of common baths for both sexes. One could have a shower, or bathe in a warm bath or submit to the exertion of a steam-bath. Afterwards one oiled one's body with fine olive oil, used perfumes and removed superfluous hair with the flame of a lamp.

On the lady's dressing table lay expensive mirrors—bright metal discs with long handles or with stands to prop them up—finely worked jewel caskets and various containers: round *aryballoi* (oil flasks), longish *alabastra* (perfume bottles), little jugs called *lekythi*, round boxes or *pyxides* and glass flasks filled with ointments, dyes, oils and scent; there were combs, mostly of ivory, and perhaps a fan, which the lady could hold graciously and coquettishly.

The application of all these gadgets and treatment cost the woman of the ancient world as much time as they cost the modern woman.

Of course it was especially the hetaerae, in their need to capitalize on their attraction, who had unearthed the secrets of the beautician's arts—who better than they knew the fear of old age? They were in the forefront of the struggle against the implacable signs of fading, against wrinkles and grey hair. Here we come to the sad side of cosmetics, which becomes in the end a crumbling anchor of hope. The cosmetic arts of women have not only aroused the admiration of men, but also their mockery and loathing.

A sober married man expresses his opinions on hetaerae as follows:

"Our wives are not painted with white lead like you and do not have cheeks coloured with mulberry juice. And when you go out in the summer, two black streaks run from your eyes down your cheeks and the sweat digs a red lead groove from cheeks to neck: your hair flopping over your face looks grey, with all that white lead in it."   (*Athen. XIII 557 foll.*)

When the young wife of Isomachus, well known to us from the pages of Xenophon, was once encountered by him with make-up on her face and wearing high-heeled shoes, she was told by her husband:

"Don't imagine your face painted red and white is dearer to me than your natural one. Just as the Gods have arranged matters so that horses like horses, oxen cows and sheep sheep, so men are convinced they like a clean human body best. This deception could at best take in strangers so that they are not aware of it, but people who are used to one another are invariably caught out when they try to deceive one another. If they get up out of bed they are either surprised without having put their make-up on, or else sweat betrays them and tears reveal their tricks and the bath exposes them quite naturally to the eyes of others."

PART II *ROME*

WOMEN AND THE LAW

"All other nations are masters of their women: we on the other hand are masters of all other nations and over us are our masters—the women."

(Plutarch, Cato the Elder, 8, 4)

The words of one of the most outstanding champions of practical Roman republicanism have been quoted because of the paradox they contain, not because they can really be regarded as an accurate description of the real situation. Cato is expressing his disapproval and launching an appeal to put an end to encroachments such as that represented by the troublesome demonstration against the *Lex Oppia*, a law passed in 215 B.C. on the limitation of expense incurred by women. And Cato's saying, "As soon as the women begin to be set alongside you as equals, they are your superiors" (*Livy, Roman History* 34, 3) was intended less as a compliment to the spontaneously demonstrated energy and political expertise of the Roman women than as honest masculine protest at an unconstitutional rebellion, which had to be nipped in the bud. In actual fact the successful protest against the *Lex Oppia* in 195 B.C. could have been a kind of signal for a movement of political emancipation for women, if it had not been prompted purely by the vanity and ostentation of the fair sex. Later at the close of the republic, when the *triumvirs* had imposed a war tax upon 1,400 of Rome's richest women, there was once more a successful display of feminine solidarity and resistance in the forum.

"Why should we pay a tax, when we do not share in the enjoyment of public office, honours and provinces, and have no part at all in the state administration, about which you are now squabbling and creating the greatest mischief?"

But seldom did such determined phalanxes of women appear on the political front of the Roman state. More often it was an individual champion, like Vergil's Camilla who enthusiastically devoted herself to matters of state, mostly through influence exerted on her men folk.

Though participation in public life secured no political rights for a woman, for she neither possessed the franchise nor could she occupy any office except that of priestess, in Rome she had a completely different relationship to the state from that of her Greek sister. The reason for this is not to be found in any greater liberality of temperament among Romans, but simply in the great respect and significance accorded to the Roman family, which in early times as a self-contained organism operated

48

as a state within a state. Even in later centuries, despite the growing process of individualization and the loosening of family ties, the family did not lose its political significance in the struggle for power. The woman was not merely an indispensable appendage of a household and the unfortunately necessary mother of its children; in a certain sense, she represented, as much as her husband did, a continuing way of life and the family's political tradition. She passed the family inheritance to her sons, and the daughter of an ancient and influential line of nobles, like Caecilia Metella, knew that she was being politically active when she gave her hand to a man like Sulla.

However, if one judges the situation of the Roman woman only in the light of the provisions of the law, one cannot avoid the impression that, at least in early times, she lived in conditions approximating slavery. But the actual picture of the life of Roman women to some extent contradicts this.

This great contradiction between the legal suppression and the conscious and respected individuality of the Roman matron is difficult for us to understand since we are accustomed to secure all our relationships on a firm basis of law, and it is therefore all the more necessary that we should not lose sight of this contradiction. The actual norms laid down by law seldom corresponded with continually changing social relationships and often became cruel fetters on the personal lives of human beings. For example, the unlimited *patria potestas* could degenerate, in the absence of definite penalties imposed by religion, into acts of the most arbitrary tyranny, until state authority imposed controls on it.

The ancient republican family was the largely sovereign household of persons and possessions, presided over by the *pater familias* as head. He possessed unlimited supreme power of life and death over members of the family, and only religious sanctions and, later, the moral supervision of the censors limited his supremacy. Nearest to him stood the *mater familias*, but even she was in his power. The maintenance of their ancestor-cult, together with the moral obligation not to allow the sacred entity of the family to be abandoned without issue, bound them together.

The demands which a peasant holding made upon the household community gave the woman her round of duties. Residing in the *atrium*, the centre of the house and not banned to a closed gynaeconitis, respected as *domina* (mistress) of slaves and servants, she managed the household affairs, brought up the children and received guests at her husband's side. She might leave the house, people respectfully made way for her in the street, even if the amusements of a Rome which has become a city—such as the circus, the theatre, the baths and the gladiatorial combats—may have passed the austere matron of the old republic by.

The legal norms never possessed the character of a completely binding system. The life of the Romans was in practice regulated by the *mores maiorum*—the inalienable customs of their ancestors, so rooted in the powerfully developed Roman consciousness of tradition that they really possessed moral force, and could be used by the state as a powerful vehicle of propaganda. Even Augustus appealed to these traditions to implement his unpopular conservative policy on marriage and the family. The honourable family lived according to these mores. They restrained the husband from unjustifiable acts of tyranny and gave the wife social dignity.

If a child was born, the father had the right to "hold it up" and thus to acknowledge it as his, otherwise it had to be exposed or got rid of in some way. By holding it up, he demonstrated his possession of the *patria potestas* over that child, that is, supreme power of life and death, and acknowledged it as a rightful heir.

A girl was brought up with a view to marriage and when her autocratic master had found a bridegroom for her, she was married. There was no fixed legal form for the marriage, which was also not liable to any state interference. It was based on the mutual consciousness that a partnership was being entered into which was to be a lifelong union. In addition to sexual maturity, which constituted the majority for both partners (girls at 12 years, boys 14 years of age) they had to have the right of *connubium* (intermarriage): this was not recognized in the case of union with near blood-relations, slaves and foreigners without Roman citizenship, or in unions between patricians and plebeians before the *Lex Canuleia* of 445 B.C.

Marriage was preceded by a betrothal. The *sponsalia* was a mutual promise of marriage entered into by the girl's father or guardian and the bridegroom. It could be made long before the marriage and later became a popular practice for making political alliances, which could then be broken off according to the prevailing political climate. The bridegroom gave the bride an iron ring, which she had to wear on the fourth finger of her left hand, as a sign of her acquiescence.

If a girl resisted marriage, she could be forced into it by her autocratic father. If she remained in his *potestas* after marriage, he had the right to interfere in her matrimonial affairs and thus represented a possible disruptive factor for the young couple. To avoid this, the father could release his daughter from his authority and place her under the authority of her husband by means of the *conventio in manum*. This transference of authority, though it mostly ran parallel with the actual marriage, was a separate legal process and could be omitted, though it rarely was at this period. If the marriage was celebrated without transfer of authority, the young wife did not legally enter the household of her husband and had no rights of inheritance there.

In the course of centuries, three forms of marriage contract emerged. The most ancient and honourable form, probably confined to patrician families, was the *confarreatio*. A solemn religious ceremony, in which ten witnesses—high priests like the Flamen Dialis and the Pontifex Maximus—participated, united the couple, who sat with covered heads on two chairs tied together and submitted to various rites, the climax of which was the sacrifice and partaking of wheat bread.

The less exclusive, but so much the commoner form of marital union, was the *coëmptio*, a fictitious bride-purchase. The third and least ceremonial form was cohabitation-*usus*: if a marriageable woman had lived for one year in her husband's house without absenting herself for longer than three days from it, her husband possessed absolute authority—*manus*—over her. According to ancient custom the woman received a dowry from her family—the *dos*—which was due to the husband, passed into his property and was looked upon as compensation for the bride's maintenance. Later, in the train of women's emancipation, marriage portions were inalienable—the wife's dowry had to be given back if the marriage was dissolved.

A woman could become *sui juris*, i.e. free of authority, by the act of *emancipatio*. Her father fictitiously sold her (*mancipatio*) to an agent who then resold (*remancipatio*) her to her father, and the latter released her by *manumissio*. Therewith she parted from her *gens* (family) and lost her right of inheritance. Later many Roman women chose this possibility to shake off their family bonds and become relatively independent.

Here we come to the third form of male authority over women—the *tutela mulierum*. Even when a woman had become *sui juris* by means of *emancipatio* or the death of her autocratic master, she had to have a protector, who had to lend her his *auctoritas* for all matters of business and legal transactions. The tutor—mostly one of her nearest *agnates*, i.e. brothers, father's brothers and their sons—was there to protect the woman's rights, to assist her in all affairs of life and manage her property without personal gain. It is this *tutela* (guardianship or protection) that gives us the best clue to the progress of women's emancipation. Though never entirely abolished, it sank into insignificance in the course of time.

If a marriage terminated in the husband's death, the wife and her children were freed of authority and the family bond lapsed. A religious regulation forbade the widow to remarry before an interval of ten months, but nothing further prevented her from entering into a new union. On the other hand, divorce was practically impossible for her and even the man could not divorce a guiltless wife without incurring religious or censorial penalties. Only serious moral delicts on the part of the wife such as adultery, attempted murder, abortion and even indulgence in wine justified the husband in putting her away. The sternness of this code is shown by the fact that in the first five centuries of Rome's history divorces were an extreme rarity; women desiring to rid themselves of their husbands preferred to poison them rather than to attempt the legal method which was for them probably impossible and taboo. But divorces became a regular practice in later republican and imperial times at any rate among the upper classes.

Politics and culture got a fresh impetus in Rome after the Punic Wars. The self-sufficient peasant economy was overshadowed by trade, and territorial expansion and the circulation of money went hand in hand with the rise of an urban culture increasingly stamped by Greek and oriental influences. During this period Rome became a world city and its republic became an empire. Scholars of jurisprudence have looked upon the last two centuries of the Republic up to the principate of Augustus and including the imperial era up to Severus Alexander (235 A.D.) as the period of pre-classical and classical law. This lays down the limits which separate ancient Roman law and the postclassical law, which was markedly influenced by Christianity, from the rise and heyday of the Roman empire.

50

This period saw the winning of greater independence for women and thereby greater participation in public life through the acquisition of an economic position guaranteed by law. At the same time the forces thus set free could not be put at the service of society in a really effective and constructive manner, since women continued to be barred from offices and honours, political rights and duties. Nevertheless the need for activity turned the Roman women ever more strongly towards life outside the home. The last years of the republic and the early imperial period witnessed an indulgence in pleasure and immorality as a safety-valve for the women of the upper classes, who had been let off the tight rein, were free from material worries and were bored.

As far as the common people were concerned, the slow loosening of family ties and the general process of individualization brought no comparable change in their way of life. They had no part in complicated income-relationships, inheritance processes and estate administration, and their wives, who were shopkeepers, seamstresses, serving-maids, etc. led a life without luxury and expense; even the stability of marriages among the lower strata of society was a clear indication of the deep gulf that separated the classes within the Roman nation.

Again it is the epitaphs that tell us of the marital fidelity and high reputation of a wife or the virtue of a departed spouse.

"Farewell, Annonia Paula, my rare wife, who would have been a model for all women had you not departed hence at the age of 33 and left your husband a terrible legacy of tears."

"She was an incomparable wife, a good mother, a venerable grandmother, chaste, pious, industrious, honest, vigorous, watchful, careful, the true wife of one man alone, a family mother of diligence and dependability."

(from: *H. Geist, Römische Grabinschriften, Munich* 1969, nos. 20, 22).

The authority-free form of marriage became commoner and prevailed after the introduction of the principate almost without exception. Limiting measures checked the patria potestas; thus a father no longer had the power to force a daughter into marriage and the family guardianships could be evaded or reduced in importance by the free choice of a protector, especially since from the Emperor Claudius' time onwards tutelage by the *agnates*

was legally abandoned. Furthermore for certain matters the *auctoritas tutoris* was no longer essential and could in case of need be demanded and received from the *praetor*. Testamentary powers, which no woman, even if *sui juris*, possessed up to Hadrian's time, could be secured by a *coëmptio testamenti faciendi gratia*, a procedure akin to emancipation between the woman and a pseudo-purchaser, who then let her go free.

Attempts were continually being made to limit the property which women might possess. Thus for example the *Lex Voconia* of 169 B.C. forbade the first census class to nominate women as heirs.

Augustus, who tried to regenerate the Roman state, attempted by means of his drastic marriage legislation to stem the moral collapse and aversion to children of many Romans, thereby paving the way for the emergence of a select elite. Thus all free-born citizens were forbidden to marry women of doubtful morality such as prostitutes, pimps, adulteresses and actresses, and members of senatorial families were forbidden to marry freedmen or women, actors and actresses, or their issue. In general marriage was made compulsory. Men between 25 and 60 and women between 20 and 50 years of age had to live in a state of legal matrimony and have at least one child. Upon the death of a partner or in the case of divorce, matrimony had once more to be entered into, the only concessions being made in favour of free-born citizens with three children, and of freedmen and -women with four. For the woman, triple maternity meant liberation from family protection and thus complete independence, whereas unmarried women forfeited the whole and childless married women half of their inheritance.

Important changes were also made in the divorce laws. However fidelity remained the absolute duty of the wife, and the husband who caught his wife in adultery was legally entitled to kill her with impunity. In the case of divorce there were now no more restrictions and the growing number of divorces bears witness to the "lack of danger" involved in this undertaking, especially since religious penalties had lost their force. A man could now divorce an innocent wife, for example because of childlessness. The consent of the family-head to the dissolution of a marriage was no longer necessary. On the other hand the *pater familias* retained the power to dissolve arbitrarily a marriage entered into by his daughter *sine manu*. Similarly, a wife had the right to leave her husband,

51

a step which, if she were in his power, was made more difficult by a certain legal procedure, but which she could insist upon after the measures adopted by Augustus. At the dissolution of the marriage, the woman's dowry had to be made available so that her maintenance was assured. The divorce process was not bound to any legal forms. A partner changed his or her address and thus dissolved the partnership, in most cases after the formal dispatch of a divorce-messenger had given notice of intention.

Yet another form of connubial partnership must be mentioned which was encouraged by the numerous marital prohibitions. It did not, it is true, possess the social prestige and full legal status of a marriage but was often entered into as a relationship and was a stable component of the Roman social fabric: concubinage. This morganatic marriage was entered into mostly by men in the higher ranks of society with women of lower origin, often in addition to their legal marriage, but rich women also lived in concubinage with men of lower social standing, for example freedmen. A freedwoman was entitled to marry but could not come under the authority—*in manu*—of her husband, who thus had no right to inherit her property, which continued to fall to her previous owner. Slave-women on the other hand had no legal right to marry and their children were "fatherless" and unfree like their mother.

In the 4th century A.D. the influence of Christianity slowly but surely began to make itself felt on Roman law. Marriage increasingly became an institution determined by moral norms. The wife could now demand conjugal fidelity from her husband and if he defaulted in this, could make it a ground for obtaining a divorce. In general the tendency was towards the indissolubility of marriage. Heavy penalties for frivolous divorce—such as lifelong banishment to a cloister or loss of all property—threatened both man and wife. The emperors intervened in the personal sphere of family life with a whole catalogue of grounds for divorce. Still the legal norms of late classical times were not at all unfavourable for the woman, even if the new Christian outlook would not and could not bring liberation in the direction of public activity.

THE ROMAN WOMAN

"Step o'er the threshold into the great world."

(Ovid, Ars Amatoria 3, 418)

There is no such thing as an ordinary Roman woman. The first thing the subject "Roman woman" does is to evoke a feeling of discomfort over the methods of assigning innumerable individuals to categories. The accurate and inaccurate, the affectionate and reverent portraits of women as well as those drawn in passion or hatred, from the pen of brilliant young poets, staid historians and biased advocates, evoke the living fascination of the originals which make us forget the two thousand years that separate them from us. They are not only living because we know their names and because their lovely images shine forth from the pages of their adorers, but because the atmosphere of Roman life can still be felt in the ruins of buildings, in roads, in the masterpieces of portraiture, in dates and inscriptions and in just those poems, speeches, biographies and histories. They all present essential features of Roman life and do not stop at the impersonal description of events and at myth but throw light upon individual destinies and the intimate details of everyday life. Whoever walks through Pompeii or reads Cicero's letters, despairs of Lesbia with Catullus or finds the centre of heaven in the Pantheon, will never feel out of touch, for past life is everywhere still palpable and real, even if seldom so terribly real as in the lava imprints of the victims of the eruption of Vesuvius of 79 A.D.

On the other hand the early period of Rome—the monarchical age and the first centuries of the republic—is obscure. It was even obscure for the Romans of classical times and when Juvenal looks back to the third century B.C. in his touching portrayal of feminine integrity he is far from evoking the "good old days" of Rome:

"Once poor, and therefore chaste, in former times
Our matrons were; no luxury found room,
In low-roofed houses, and bare walls of loam;
Their hands with labour hardened while 'twas light,
And frugal sleep supplied the quiet night;
While pinched with want, their hunger held them straight,
When Hannibal was hovering at the gate."

J. Dryden   *(Juvenal, Satires 6, 285—290)*

At that time the Roman lady was above all *mater familias*. As active mistress of the house she sat at the loom among her maids, gave orders in the *Atrium* and received hospitably the friends of the family. She was dignified and stern and obeyed her husband, just as children, servants and slaves obeyed her. The holy hearth-fire and the gods of the family were in her keeping, as was the upbringing of her children. Usually several women lived in one household; the husband's sisters and the mother-in-law aided the young wife.

Her wedding was the most brilliant festival in her feminine life. When a suitable day had been fixed, (the months of March, May, and June were not customary for weddings, according to the complicated sacred calendar of the Romans) the bride-to-be had to say farewell to her childhood and youth. She dedicated her toys to the gods and exchanged her girl's robe *(toga praetexta)* for her bridal dress, the *tunica recta*, held together by a woollen girdle twisted into Hercules knots. Her head was covered by her bride's red veil-cloth *(flammeum)*. Her hair was divided into six strands with a sharp iron instrument bent at the end, each strand was tied up with a ribbon and a home-made chaplet of flowers completed her beauty treatment and ceremonial appearance.

If the marriage took the form of a *confarreatio*, the solemn rites already mentioned were celebrated; the formula "ubi tu Gaius, ego Gaia" was repeated and meant: "Where you are master of the house, I am the mistress."

Then a married woman, *pronuba*, joined the hands of the couple together. After numerous sacrifices to the gods began the *cena*, the great wedding feast in the bride's house. With the evening star the last part of the marriage festivities approached, the *deductio in domum*, the removal of the bride to the house of her husband. Now she was theatrically torn out of her mother's arms by the bridegroom. The tearful farewells were however assuaged by the musicians, torchbearers, relatives and friends male and female who accompanied the marriage procession. The fescennine verses were sung, and rough jokes were shouted out. The bridegroom scattered walnuts among the children. Three boys whose parents were still alive escorted the bride. In their hands they held hawthorn torches and carried distaff and spindle into the new home for her. The young bride took up her new home by anointing the doorposts and decorating them with bands of woollen material, before her husband lifted her over the threshold and, in accordance with cult rites initiated her into the water and fire of his house. Only then was the bridegroom allowed to receive her from the hand of a *pronuba*, upon the marriage-bed prepared in the *Atrium*.

Catullus has preserved the ancient customs for us in his "Wedding Song":

Lady in a Roman butcher's shop

"Here is your husband's stately home;
See how blessed 'twill be for you,
Only let it your service do—
Hymen, ho! Hymenaeus, ho!
Hymen, ho! Hymenaeus!

Till the distant day when age
Shakes the grey locks on your tremulous brow,
And bends your head in assent to all—
Hymen, ho! Hymenaeus, ho!
Hymen, ho! Hymenaeus!

Over the threshold set your foot—
Clad in a golden, lucky shoe,
Pass through the brightly polished door—
Hymen, ho! Hymenaeus, ho!
Hymen, ho! Hymenaeus!

See how your husband on his couch
Of Tyrian hue reclines and waits
And yearns for the coming of his bride—
Hymen, ho! Hymenaeus, ho!
Hymen, ho! Hymenaeus!

Just like yours his heart burns deep,
Deep inside him burns his love,
Buries its fires in his inmost breast—
Hymen, ho! Hymenaeus, ho!
Hymen, ho! Hymenaeus!

Boy, let go of the tender arm,
Let the beautiful bride go free,
Free for her husband's fond embrace—
Hymen, ho! Hymenaeus, ho!
Hymen, ho! Hymenaeus!

Faithful women, ever revered
By faithful greybeard husbands, up!
Set the bride on her marriage-bed—
Hymen, ho! Hymenaeus, ho!
Hymen, ho! Hymenaeus!"

(Catullus, Carmina 61, 156—190)

The Roman woman remained a housewife—*mater familias*—for hundreds of years even if she took less and less active part in manual work, at any rate in the rich houses of the upper class.

Tibullus, it is true, dreams of rural bliss at the side of his Delia, but she prefers the summer sunshine at the elegant spa of Baiae:

"Delia (said I) will guard the reaper's band;
Delia will keep, when hinds unload the vine,
The choicest grapes for me, the richest wine:
My flocks she'll count, and oft will sweetly deign
To clasp some prattler of my menial train:
With pious care will load each rural shrine,
For ripened crops a golden sheaf assign,
Cates for my fold, rich clusters for my vine:
No, no domestic care shall touch my soul;
You, Delia, reign despotic o'er the whole!"

(James Grainger, 1812)   (Tibullus, I, 5, 21—30)

In the third century B.C., after Rome had shown herself a world power in the confrontation with the sea-power of Carthage, changes occurred in the Roman family, and the practical intelligence of the Roman woman also entered new spheres. Greek education and the fine arts perfected the woman's elementary education. In addition to severity and respectability, the Roman matron began to acquire a taste for domination; in many marriages a rich dowry ensured dominance for the wife, made her demanding and a regular pest to her husband.

"The dowry I brought you was greater far
Than what you had in fortune. So I say
You'll have to give me purple robes and gold,
Mules, muleteers, and serving men and women,
Pages to run my errands, and a coach
To take me where I want."

(Plautus, Pot of Gold, 3, 10)

But emancipation entailed great danger for the civic and patrician woman. Not that a whole burden of responsibilities would fall on her, or that she would have to prove herself in profession and in public life to be the equal of man. On the contrary: boredom, leisure and wealth came to mold her character, and even the most careful education was not enough to help the girl come to grips with her actual social helplessness and inactivity. It is thus not surprising that the ancient standard of morals was turned on its head and excesses, including cruelty and crime, were to be numbered among the great lady's pastimes?

While Juvenal cannot be regarded as an impartial judge and his sixth satire may be as much an indication of the writer's malice as of the real depravity of the Roman ladies, it remains unquestioned that his satires have a basis in fact.

"One's shoulders break the rod, another's are
  Red from the whip, a third from the cat-o-nine-tails;
  The floggers are commissioned by the year.
  So goes the thrashing while she smears her face,
  Listens to gossips, looks at the broad hem
  Of a brocaded robe—on goes the thrashing
  While she reads through the daily news—on goes
  The thrashing, till she thunders at the tired
  Floggers "Get out!"—at last the thrashing's done."

                          (Juvenal, Satires VI, 478—85)

The Roman lady devoted much time and labour to the care of her face and the elegance of her dress, but we shall return to this later. She by no means exhausted her ambitions on her physical appearance, but made ever bolder inroads into the realm of the spirit and of art. Since the mother of the Gracchi, Cornelia, had made Greek education socially acceptable in a certain sense for women, too, the number of more or less serious, clever or even pretentious female adepts of erudition had risen rapidly.

Here, in dealing with his hated subject, Juvenal uses tones as strident as those of the lady who becomes the bore of the feast:

"But of all plagues, the greatest is untold;
  The book-learned wife, in Greek and Latin bold;
  The critic-dame, who at her table sits,
  Homer and Virgil quotes, and weighs their wits,
  And pities Dido's agonising fits.
  She has so far the ascendant of the board,
  The prating pedants put not in one word;
  The man of law is nonplussed in his suit,
  Nay, every other female tongue is mute.
  Hammers, and beating anvils, you would swear,
  And Vulcan, with his whole militia, there."

J. Dryden   (Juvenal, VI, 434—41)

In the affectionate description of his wife the younger Pliny has given us a contrasting picture. Here culture becomes a firm bond between the partners, not a hollow-sounding showpiece. Pliny writes to her aunt:

"She possesses exceptional intelligence and is a splendid housekeeper; she loves me tenderly, a certain proof of her chastity! In addition there is her liking for the sciences, one result of her love for me. She has my writings, reads them constantly and even learns them by heart. How nervous and anxious she is when I have to address the court, how great her joy when it's all over! She summons people to tell them how much applause and acclamation I have aroused, and how my case has gone. When on occasions I read out something to an audience, she sits nearby, behind a curtain, and drinks in my praise with the most eager ears. She sings and plays my verses on the zither without any instruction but that of love, which is the best teacher. This is the source of my confident hope that our unity will be unbreakable and will increase daily. For she does not love my youth or my person, which is transient and subject to old age, but my reputation."

                          (Pliny the Younger, Letters IV, 19)

Plutarch said of Cicero's wife Terentia "was not exactly a gentle, timorous character but an ambitious woman" (Cicero, 20), but Cicero himself is said to have remarked that "she interested herself much more in his political affairs than he let himself be interested in her household matters." The letters of the exile to the wife who had stayed behind in Rome are filled with instructions for the carrying out of delicate missions and demonstrate his confidence in Terentia's political and practical wisdom.

With his brilliant characterization of Sempronia, who was implicated in the Catiline conspiracy, Sallust illuminates a female personality of great complexity—a woman who united beauty, charm, grace, culture and artistic ability with recklessness and unscrupulousness:

"More than once she had committed crimes which called for the audacity of a man. With respect to her origins and beauty as well as in her position as the wife of a respected man and the mother of children, she was singularly blessed by fate. She was well-read in Greek and Latin literature; she could play and dance more artistically than a respectable woman needs to do and had much knowledge of matters that go to make up a life among admirers. On any and every occasion decency and morals had to take a back seat. It was difficult to decide whether she spared her property less or her reputation. She burned with such sensuality that she seduced men more often then she allowed them to seduce her. She had often broken her word, repudiated her debts and proved capable of murder—so low had she been brought by dissipation and penury. And all the time she was a woman of great intellectual capabilities. She could write verses, be witty and behave herself in company either demurely and daintily

56

or impudently; in brief, she was a woman of cheerful, appealing disposition."

(Sallust, Catiline Conspiracy, 25)

Though household economy, family politics, religious festivals and literary bacchanalian revels, games, theatres, the circus, the social duties of representation and of gossip give the impression of providing a full and varied life, we cannot have a complete picture of the Roman lady without considering love—in all its forms. The heart-rending love of young Sulpicia; the numerous extravagances of Clodia-Lesbia, Cynthia, Delia, the dissolute sensualities of proud ladies, stealing the thunder from the brothel-girls by having themselves registered as practitioners of the trade. Adultery was the society game, and one had only to decide whether to make secrecy and the fear of discovery into a spice for pleasure or to agree mutually, as Juvenal informed us,

"That you can do whatever takes your fancy,
And I'll not stint myself in any way."

(Juvenal, VI, 280-1)

Catullus, Propertius and Tibullus have their joys and sorrows not from young girls who wish to be made honest women, but from married ladies of the upper class, who alongside, before and after the poets entertain other lovers. Their affairs have been the occasion of wonderful love-poems, with the woman depicted as goddess despite her dissolute and inconstant behaviour, irresistible in her sensual enjoyment of life.

With Propertius we accompany Cynthia in her carriage to Praeneste, to Tibur and Lanuvium, we sit with her fencer-friend in a pony-trap, which she, leaning right forward over the pole, drives at breakneck speed through disreputable places past Lanuvium to the scene of the annual celebration of the dragon's victim, we meet her again in the elegant spa of Baiae, where upon the Hercules mole looking out to sea she forgets Rome and her lover, so that the latter warns her:

"Leave this corrupted Baiae speedily,
This shore, the cause of many a divorce,
This enemy to virtuous womanhood,
And cursed be Baiae, ruinous to love!"

(Propertius, Elegies 1, 12, 27—30)

The gulf between street walker and married woman, which yawned wide in Greece despite the smartness and brilliance of the hetaera-class, was more a matter of property than of conduct in Rome. Among some families, life was still governed by the traditional code of morals, but adultery, love-affairs and frequent divorce were everyday matters.

Juvenal bemoans the behaviour of a newly wedded wife:

"Thus the she-tyrant reigns, till, pleased with change,
Her wild affections to new empires range;
Another subject-husband she desires;
Divorced from him, she to the first retires,
While the last wedding-feast is scarcely o'er,
And garlands hang yet green upon the door.
So still the reckoning rises; and appears
In total sum, eight husbands in five years.
The title for a tombstone might be fit,
But that it would too commonly be writ."

J. Dryden   (Juvenal VI, 224—230)

Ovid betrays to us the places where Amor is up to his wild tricks: the shadowed colonnades, decorated with ancient paintings; but in the forum too, especially at the Public Games, the best opportunities presented themselves:

"Go hunting round the theatre—you'll find
A richer booty than you've ever prayed for"

(Ars amat. I, 89—90)

It was especially clowns and actors who enjoyed the favour of the ladies, and were only exceeded in this by the brutal attractiveness of gladiators, who even succeeded in enticing the wives of senators away from the path of virtue. The lady went on foot or dallied, lolling on the cushions of her litter, with her admirers.

But let us leave the sophisticated love-bouts and preliminaries into which Ovid and Horace initiated the inquisitive Roman public and listen to a much sadder tale of everyday life.

Rome did not exist by virtue of the lords and ladies whose riches were rooted in the work of their hordes of slaves. Rome became the Roman Empire through its wars, which made husbands into legionaries and often kept them away from hearth and home for years. Loneliness and war-widowhood were the regular fate of Roman women. Especially for the class of small tradesmen and peasants the gap left by husbands, sons and brothers often meant the collapse of their livelihood, bringing poverty and misery to wives and children. Long letters had to bridge the distances and keep the scene of domestic loneliness before the mind's eye of the man away at the wars. But when had the lamentations of those who were left behind ever been able to put an end to war?

Propertius wrote for the wife of a Roman soldier:

"Arethusa sends these requests to her Lycotas, if you can still be mine, who are often so far away. If you read these lines and if some of them are smudged and illegible, my tears are to blame for the blots. Or should an unsteady letter puzzle you, it is a sign that my hand has grown tired....

Accursed be he who split the palisade from the innocent tree, who made complaining horns from the raucous ivory....

Tell me, do not your shoulders become chafed under their armour, does not the lance rub sore your hand, that is unaccustomed to war?...

Where shall I go? It is only for you that the Phoenician purple adorns me, only for you that the clear crystal bedecks my hands. All here is dumb and silent. All too rarely at the Calends does one maid, who is used to it, open the shrine of the Lares. Dear only to me is the whine of the little dog, Glaucis, who now takes your place in my bed....

But may you conquer the sons of Parthia and may a lance follow in honour the horses of the triumphant warrior! But preserve inviolate the bond of our bed— only on this condition will I welcome you home. And when I take your arms to dedicate them at the Capena gate, I will inscribe thereon "From a wife grateful for the safe return of her husband."

(Propertius, Elegies 4, 3)

Within the confines of Rome's tenement blocks, which often threatened to collapse due to the thoughtless rapacity of the builders, the life of the ordinary woman was anything but entertaining and frivolous. She had her good times, it is true, at the numerous public displays. In the press of the amphitheater or on the back rows of the circus, amidst the rough jokes of the Atellan farces and at the spectacular triumphal processions, she had her share of Rome's life, which in general took no notice of her but couldn't exist without her—the mother of the Populus Romanus. In general however, everyday life was a burden to her as to all poor mothers of families all over the world, bringing her a series of worries about children and about the work that secured her family its daily bread. Freedwomen and female slaves worked as fishmongers, barley-sellers, silk-weavers, lime-burners, clothes-menders, spinsters, ironing-women, as midwives and nurses, or as hairdressers, lady's maids, bath-attendants, but also as stenographers and doctors, singers, beaters of cymbals and actresses. All these occupations are mentioned in epitaphs. Papyrus documents from Ptolemaic Egypt under the Romans tell us about the nursing profession. About twenty nursing contracts bear witness to an institution which was widespread in Rome and in the Hellenistic States.

"The subject of a legal business agreement in the nursing contracts was the transference of a baby for the purpose of care and feeding to a slave woman or even to a free woman. Thus these services are rendered both by the owners of female slaves and also by free women, these latter always under the wing of their family protector, who on occasions also stood as guarantor for them." *(J. Hermann, Zeitschrift der Savigny-Stiftung für Rechtsgeschicht 76, 492).*

The contract committed the nurse to take the baby into her house, to feed and care for it. She was not allowed to have sexual intercourse or to feed a second child. Every three months she was interviewed by her contract-partner—the contract was usually for a two-year period—who checked up on the fulfilment of her duties. She received money and wages in kind, usually the oil that she needed for the care of the body. If the baby entrusted to her was a slave-child and died, she had to pay compensation, i.e. if she were a slave, her owner had to "lift up" another child and then hand it over to the contract-partner after an agreed interval.

The life of a slave-woman was determined by her conditions. Trained to a trade, occupied at home or on a farm she was dependent on the whim of her owner but could reach positions of some respect within her own class. Such a position was attained by the stewardess, the partner of a steward or farm-manager. Cato concerned himself in detail with the duties of such a woman:

"She should be satisfied with the man her master has given her and he should make her fear him. She must not be too fond of luxury. She must also avoid much contact with neighbours and other women and not invite them to visit her. She ought not to go anywhere to eat and she must under no circumstances be a lounger. She must also know that she may not sacrifice or have sacrifice made for her. She must clean the manor daily and before she goes to bed she must clean the hearth and turn it round. On holidays she should lay a wreath on the hearth and on such days pray to the family god for prosperity. She must also see to it that the slave family is well fed. She must keep many hens so that there are sufficient eggs, also dried pears, hawthorn berries, stewed hawthorn berries, pears and grapes in tubs and quinces in wine jugs, she should bury fresh Praeneste nuts in jars in the earth and she must also have Campanian apples in barrels. And she must see to it that good flour is ground."

(Cato, De agricultura 143)

Columella (*De re rustica* XII), too, turns his attention to the stewardess. She should see to it that all the household utensils are kept in their proper place. She must pay particular attention to the foodstuffs, none of which must be allowed to go bad. When the weather is bad she should not work outdoors. Then in the house she must work with the carded wool. She must make clothes for herself, for the steward and for the slaves. In this way she saves her master money. If a slave says he is ill, she questions him about his aches and pains and takes him into the sick-room, and does this even when a slave is merely overtired; then after a few days he will be completely fit for work. She may only sit around when she herself is really tired. She must keep an eye on the weaving-shed, on the kitchen and the cellar and the stables, but above all on the sick-room, which must be properly cleaned and ventilated. Then she must look after everything that comes into her hands, especially fruit and crockery. She must supervise the winecellar master and the cellar and kitchen masters. She must be present when fruit is brought in. At the sheep-shearing she looks on and takes care of the wool. She orders the domestic servants to polish the iron plates, spoons, knives and forks till they gleam. They must also spread the table. She only distributes foodstuffs to the slaves when her husband is absent. She should not be too young, not ugly but also not too beautiful.

RELIGION AND CULT

Nearness to the gods was an integral part of everyday life in Rome. This religious feeling, deeply rooted in life, had its origin like all religion and magic in the search of an explanation for the apparently arbitrary processes of life and nature, the meaning of which was wrapped in enigmatic obscurity. In order to acquire some power over these mysterious forces, power which might serve as a basis for personal security, people made them into immediate neighbours, personified and named them; by this means a relationship was created on the basis of which dealings were possible.

The Romans made the utilitarian principle of trade the basis of their relations with the gods. They themselves divided time into '*ferial*', into '*dies fasti*' and '*dies nefasti*', meaning "useful" and "belonging to the gods," and in every prayer outlined the demand to be paid for by sacrifice. To avoid gaps in the system of communication with the powers of destiny, they resorted to a vast number of personifications, which appeared alongside the chief established Italic and Etruscan gods. The hellenization of Rome and the expansion of the empire brought a whole series of foreign cults to Rome, which led to ecstasies and mystical excesses not characteristic of the indigenous, almost sober, religious practices.

The women had an active share in all religious matters. In private life at home the Romans at their mealtimes always thought of their *Penates* (household gods). All important occasions in the family and out on the fields were solemnly accompanied by sacrifices and prayers in order not to disturb the harmonious relationship with the wide variety of gods. At the beginning of June the housewife made a sacrifice to the hearth-goddess Vesta and the daughter of the house made an offering every day to the special guardian deity of the house, the Lar. At the Calends of every month special attention was due to him: servant-girls opened his cupboard and presented an offering to him.

Although women participated in almost all state acts of religious worship, they also possessed for their own special interests a whole series of their own female divinities, to the service of whom they devoted themselves with great zeal, often with all men excluded. Juno was the goddess primary. As Juno Lucina she aided women in childbirth and after a successful delivery thanks were offered to her in the shape of a sacrifice of food set out on a table in the *atrium*. The great festival to Juno was the *Matronalia* on the first of March. Only respectable married women were allowed to appear in the sanctuary

"Italia" represented as goddess of fertility

of the goddess in the Esquiline and pray for further happy years of marriage and the blessing of many children, while the men brought presents to them. As Juno Lanuvia the goddess watched over the chastity of women and virgins; prostitutes were forbidden to touch her altar. A special feature of Lanuvium was the "virgin test." A dragon, or rather a snake in all probability, decided about the chastity of the girls by eating or rejecting a mouthful of food offered to it.

Propertius describes this ancient fertility rite:

"Long has Lanuvium been in the keeping of an ancient dragon, here—an hour of rare repose is a boon— here, where a holy stone disappears in the dark abyss, which a virgin enters (Girl, think on it, ere thou goest!), when the worshipped dragon in his hunger demands his annual sacrifice and rears himself up out of the earth with a deep hissing. At this ceremony the girls that are sent down grow pale as they blindly trust their hands to the maw of the reptile. But it takes the morsels if a virgin offers them to it, and then the basket in the virgin's hand trembles of itself. If they have been chaste, they return home to the bosom of their parents, and their countrymen cry "This will be a fruitful year!" *(Propertius, Elegies 4, 83foll.)*

The ancient festival of the Caprotine Nones was also reserved for the fair sex. Mock-battles by serving girls, squibs and lampoons, the fig-tree with its fruit that symbolizes the female genitals all had a part in the rites of the ancient fertility cult celebrated at this festival on 7th July. The goat is very closely associated with the goddess and even at the *Lupercalia* held on 15th February the fertilizing function of this animal plays a key part. At this festival in honour of Faunus the priests or *Luperci* cut strips from the hide of a he-goat that had been sacrificed and with these they ran around making a great noise and lashing at anyone who got in their way. Women of course deliberately ran into them, believing that the blows they received had power to make them fertile and give them an easy confinement.

Under Greek influence the ancient Roman goddess Fauna became the *Bona Dea* (good goddess), a powerful female divinity honoured with secret rites. At her festival at the beginning of December, the exclusion of men was the most stringent injunction and any transgression in this respect was to be rigorously punished. A famous scandal occurred in 62 B.C., when P. Clodius

Pulcher desecrated Caesar's house in order to secure an assignation with Caesar's wife at a time when the most respected matrons in Rome had gathered for the festival of the *Bona Dea*. A sacrifice of such importance for the well-being of the whole state was held in the house of a high official and present at the festival were the city's most distinguished ladies and also the Vestal virgins, the chaste, privileged state priestesses of Vesta. The festal chamber was decorated with vines, the celebrants drank wine, which was distributed as if it were milk, and ate pork, the flesh of the sacrificial animal, while the atmosphere grew merry with song and dance. Many a politically necessary omen was observed, cleverly staged by ambitious wives, at the holy hearth during the festival of *Bona Dea*. This goddess, the Greek Damia, also possessed healing powers. At her sanctuary on the slope of the Aventine there was a kind of medical station organized by women, who were *sacerdotes*, *magistrae* or *ministrae*.

Diana of Aricia and Diana of Nemi drew women from all over Italy into their sanctuaries. Pictorial representations of genitals and statuettes of mothers and children point to functions assigned to sex. This goddess, who was also the patroness of slaves, had a temple on the Aventine, whose foundation day, 13th August, was celebrated by women paying particular attention to their coiffure. Positioned near her was Egeria, goddess of birth, whose kindred sisters the *Mater Matuta* and the *Fortuna Virginalis* were honoured in the *Forum Boarium*. The *Fortuna* sanctuary on the Via Latina was reserved for the *univirae*, women who had only been married once, and the same is true of Pudicitia, protectress of conjugal chastity.

With the *Cerealia*, of plebeian origin, we meet with Hellenic influence upon the cult practices of the Romans. The mysteries of Ceres in Greece were the model and the inspiration for the Roman ritual. Austere rules for chastity, a taboo on the eating of bread, and wine-libations had to be observed by the believers, who appeared in white garments and special headdress at the representation of the Persephone myth.

The cult of Isis, imported from Egypt, had a powerful hold on the minds of women, so easily inspired by dramatic representation. The mystery of the death and resurrection of Osiris-Serapis, the lamentation and rejoicing of Isis, mother of gods, seized the imagination of girls and women of all classes and induced them to observe week-long abstinence and tormenting ceremonies at the behest of the priests:

"Through ice they beat, and plunge into the stream,
  If so the God has warned them in a dream.
  Weak in their limbs, but in devotion strong,
  On their bare hands and feet they crawl along
  A whole field's length, the laughter of the throng.
  Should Io (Io's priest, I mean) command
  A pilgrimage to Meroe's burning sand,
  Through deserts they would seek the secret spring,
  And holy water for lustration bring."

J. Dryden   *(Juvenal II, 6, 522 foll.)*

Magna Mater, *Bellona*, *Dea Suria*, with their partly cruel, partly spectacular rites and processions also fired the religious fervour of women. In addition to established cults, there were the swarms of astrologers, miracle-mongers from the East, sorceresses and female poisoners and mediums from Germany who swindled many a woman out of her property, hurled her into the path of vice and crime and ruined her family life. The multifarious love-magicians seem to have had the most devastating effects. They were dangerous not only for the unfortunate patients, to whom they often brought death or protracted maladies, but also for small boys, since the sorceress often needed substances from their poor tormented bodies for her elixirs. With the aid of female poisoners—we only need to think of Locusta, the intimate of the Empress Agrippina—people pursued political aims and tried to combat sickness and death.

Judaism and Christianity found many adherents among the female members of families and many a divorce had its origin in religious grounds.

HEROINES IN MYTH AND HISTORY

"I have no intention either of substantiating or confuting those accounts, coming down to us more in the guise of poetic creation than of verifiable evidence, of circumstances alleged to be connected with either the ancient or more recent construction of the city."

This is how Livy in the preface to his historical works justifies his own lively imagination, which has created for us from a host of facts and myths a gripping and vivid fresco of Roman history. It was not an age of the gods, though the Vestal virgin, Rhea Silva, maintained that Mars himself was the father of the twin brothers that founded the city. For a Roman, living in the crisis-shaken first century B.C., it was an exciting story: its rational train of cause and effect, its gripping stories of individual destinies, and interactions of political and social upheavals perhaps shed a new and clearer light upon the evils of his own age. History is told in the form of stories, the resolution of the historical process into small parts crystallizes in many cases around a key figure, who starts the ball rolling even if only through his or her passive existence.

This is the case with Verginia, a beautiful, chaste citizen's daughter, who was unlucky enough to arouse the desire of the decemvir Appius Claudius, who engineered a lawsuit that mocked all sense of law and morals in order to gain possession of the girl as a slave. *(Livy 3, 44, 47 foll.)*

A human tragedy unfolds before our eyes as her affianced bridegroom and her despairing father are forced to submit to the judgement, and only death at the hands of her father spares her the road to slavery and dishonour. This justifiable murder of a daughter gave the signal for a popular uprising which removed the dictatorship of the decemvirs in Rome.

Historical fact or historical fiction—in the end it is all one. The woman is sacrificed, a piteous symbol of helpless chastity, on the altar of an inviolable moral code.

Even earlier another model of feminine virtue and worth, Lucretia, had wiped out the shame of her ravishing by the king's son, Sextus Tarquinius, by a heroic suicide. She bequeathed to her husband and his friends the obligation to avenge her, a task which grew from the punishment of an individual crime into a national event, the overthrow of royal despotism in Rome. Once more a woman pictured in sharp outlines and endowed with the ability to act independently stood on the threshold of a political upheaval, acted as the lever that launched the landslide—and yet stood right outside the political and historical situation.

Even the ambitious Tanaquil, wife of a Tarquin, only started the ball rolling when she brought the subsequent king, Lucius Tarquinius Priscus, into the young city of Rome, which still had room for the energy of young people, and pointed out to him the omens, thus raising his expectations and fastening his gaze upon the royal crown, which was later to be taken over—again from the hand of Tanaquil—by Servius Tullius.

One special category of history-making women, the heroine of politics, rose above the limitations of her station in the whirlpool of events and become a saviour of the people. In the story of the Roman girl, Cloelia, the "true" happening is very questionable, but for the Romans this heroine was the very embodiment of female courage and patriotism. In an audacious and highly dangerous flight across the Tiber, Cloelia escaped from the Etruscan King Porsena, into whose hands she had been delivered as a hostage. The Romans, however, had to return her to him but with extraordinary courage she was able to change the mind of the besieging Etruscan, who released her and in recognition of her patriotic self-lessness handed over to her a number of Roman hostages.

The modern world has been reminded by Brecht of the historical legend of the renegade Roman, Coriolanus, who stood before Rome at the head of the Volsci but changed his mind in answer to the prayers of the Roman women led by his mother, Veturia, and his wife, Volumnia. A son's obligations and political argumentation of the patriotic Veturia averted the onslaught upon the city.

In the second century B.C. the confusion of legend, myth and history begins to clear. The eyes of posterity can look upon the life of Cornelia, the mother of the Gracchi, as rooted in historical fact. The tradition of austerity, the monumental strength of the patrician character has survived in her. For Plutarch Cornelia was:

"... at her most admirable when she remembered her sons, without pain and tears, and in answer to questions put to her, related their deeds and their martyrdoms as if they had been some men or other of ancient times. For this reason she seemed to some to have lost her mind through old age and the enormity of her loss and to have become emotionally impervious to her sons' sad fates. But these people have themselves no sense of the great human power, that lies in a fine char-acter, noble birth and distinguished education, to re-move all traces of pain."   (*Plutarch, C. Gracchus 19*)

Cornelia was the daughter of the Philhellene, Scipio Africanus the Elder, and granddaughter of Aemilius Paulus, married to the tribune of the people Tiberius Sempronius Gracchus, who though a political opponent was a personal admirer of her father. At his death in 153 B.C. she had attained such celebrity in the Hellenistic world that the King of Egypt, Ptolemy VIII, Euergetos II, offered to make her his wife. She possessed an excellent Greek education, was a master of rhetoric such as no other woman was and corresponded with philosophers, scientists and distinguished men of affairs; her house was one of the social centers of the city. Fragments of letters, however, show that she was very human, and suffered as a mother would who, with her political acumen foresaw the ruin of her sons and sought to prevent it, but was powerless to do so. She must have been unusually popular, anticipating the eminent position of later Empresses.

The last century B.C. brought civil war and the struggle for power within two triumvirates. This marks out the arena which became the scene of activity of women hungry for power and love, like Caecilia Metella, Terentia (the wife of Cicero), the Catilinarians, Sempronia and Fulvia, Servilia (mother of Caesar's murderer, Brutus), Caesar's daughter Julia, Mucia Tertia, the virago Fulvia (wife of Mark Antony) and Augustus' magnanimous sister, Octavia. By means of their personal contacts they influenced politics to a greater or lesser degree, stood forth as independently as the men did, for example, as Fulvia did in the Perusian war, or they patiently submitted to the role of victim.

In addition to both sincere and disingenuous female figures in the emperor's entourage, the imperial age once more witnessed the emergence of real heroines. In the gruesome era of proscriptions and prosecutions for *lèse majesté* especially under Tiberius, Claudius and Nero, there were women who stood faithfully by their husbands, when the latter were condemned or driven to death, and provided shining examples of courage, self-sacrifice and uncompromising loyalty. The stories of Arria, of her daughter of the same name and of her granddaughter Fannia are recounted with honour both by the younger Pliny and by Tacitus.

Pliny writes to Nepos:

"I have made the observation that among the deeds and speeches of glorious men and women some are more famous but others are greater. This opinion of mine was confirmed yesterday by the story told by Fannia. She is the granddaughter of that famous Arria who by her very example taught her husband to face death with equanimity. She related to me other things about her grandmother, no less heroic but less well known. I think you will read this story with the same admiration as that with which I heard it. It seemed that her husband, Caecina Paetus, and her son both lay dying of a fatal illness. The son died—he had been a youth of exceptionally fine appearance and morals, loved by his parents not less for his unusual qualities as for being their son. The mother took care of the corpse and organized the burial so secretly that her husband noticed nothing. Indeed, every time he came into her bedroom, she made out that the son was alive and improving. Often when he enquired what the boy was doing, she answered that he had slept well and eaten with appetite. But as soon as the long-suppressed tears got the upper hand of her and broke out, she went out and gave way to her sorrow. When she had quietened down again, she came back with dry eyes and a quiet manner, as if she had left her sorrow outside the door. Truly that deed is excellent, to draw steel, plunge it in the breast, tear out the dagger and hand it to her husband with the almost divine words, "Paetus, it doesn't hurt." But when she said and did this she had visions of fame and immortality. How much greater it is to hide tears, to conceal sorrow and to continue to play the mother after the death of a son, without the prospect of immortality, without the reward of fame ..." *(Pliny the Younger, Letters 3, 16)*

Caecina Paetus had participated in a fruitless conspiracy against the Emperor Claudius, his son-in-law was condemned to death by Nero, and Arria the younger was ready to follow her husband's example but was induced to change her mind in order to stand by her daughter Fannia. This latter lady, too, several times accompanied her husband, Helvidius Priscus, into exile, and after his execution her courageous championship of her husband brought her the confiscation of her estate and renewed exile.

Pliny writes of this Fannia:

"How pleasant, how nice and obliging she is and, something which seldom goes with it, how affectionate and honourable at the same time! We can in the future hold her up as an example to our women and even to men she will be a pattern of steadfastness!"

(Pliny the Younger, 7, 19)

THE EMPRESSES

Empresses were principally the decorative symbols of the rule of their husbands. Only a few of them made the traditional dignity of their office into a showcase for their personalities. The obligations of an empress-role hampered individual mobility, at any rate when the monarchy was hereditary and an empress was expected to produce an heir. During the later phases of development, when one-man rule began to develop from principate to despotism, the Roman empresses became legitimate partners in the power of an imperial house.

At the time of its institution the principate of Augustus in no way implied the initiation of a ruling dynasty. Augustus' wife Livia was well advised to live according to the old Roman standards of austerity and moderation and not on the model of hellenistic monarchs' wives, since she did not wish to arise the suggestion of a new royal domination, which had proved so fatal to Julius Caesar. In Rome there was no ready-made niche for the newly elected "Empress". Four changes of throne came and went without any successor being named before Claudius' wife, Julia Agrippina, advanced to the position of recognized co-regent and gave the Roman people the spectacle of oriental pomp whenever she appeared in public. Augustus remained the prisoner of his own legislation; the banishment of his only daughter, Julia, and later also of his granddaughter of the same name is to be explained more on grounds of political expediency than as a matter of the outraged father's troubled conscience against her immoral behaviour.

In terms of power, Livia, third wife to Augustus, marked out the path her successors were to tread with less moderation and therefore less felicity. Controversy has raged on the extent of her real influence on Augustus' policy; but there is no doubt about the high esteem which Augustus entertained for her throughout a happy marriage that lasted fifty years. On all important matters the Princeps consulted his "Ulysses in petticoats," as the irreverent Gaius, later the Emperor Caligula, characterized his great-grandmother, and we are told that Augustus prepared himself for his conferences with Livia with the aid of written notes. She accompanied him on all his long journeys and, as a thoughtful wife, is said to have taken live goats with her on board ship in order always to have milk on hand for the frail Augustus. The numerous acts of homage to Livia that were inspired by Augustus she had to share in part with his favourite sister Octavia. Among the honours she received were the conferment of sacrosanctity and the right to have her image on coins, the privilege of being the only woman to dine with Augustus in the Concordia temple, her adoption, through Augustus' will, into the family of the Julii, and above all her elevation to *Augusta* by which she was designed co-regent with her husband's successor. These honors confirmed the social institution of the ruling consort as well as Livia's personal position of influence.

And Livia knew how to take her chances and play the role allotted to her with bravura. Thanks to her own large fortune, which she administered personally, she was able to surround herself with a court of dependents and favourites. She held receptions every morning, which were reported in the daily journal of Rome. For the rest she knew how to hang on to her good fortune by bearing in mind the following maxims:

"I myself lived in all modesty and honour, did everything to suit him [Augustus] with pleasure, never interfered unasked in his affairs, never stuck my nose into his love-affairs but always acted as if I had not noticed anything." (*Dio Cassius 58, 2*)

Her domain was the family politics of the Julians and Claudians; and while she had no influence upon the family disasters caused by the early death of the prospective heirs to the throne, the bloody family feud was put off until her death despite the internal tensions, above all between the ambitious family of Germanicus' widow Agrippina, and her son Tiberius.

It was not until the times of Tiberius that blood flowed, not only within the ruling house itself, but also in the ranks of the supporters of the various rival groups. With her passion for domination, Livia was a nuisance to Tiberius, who was almost sixty years old when he ascended the throne on the death of Augustus. Tiberius had little joy of women, at least in marriage, after he had had to dissolve his short, happy union with Vipsania for political reasons in favour of a marriage with Augustus' daughter, Julia. He remained unmarried and embittered after Julia's unhappy end, his only female helpmate being his sister-in-law, Antonia.

During the reign Caligula, the immoral great-grandson of Livia, who was in love with oriental sensuality and morals, women began again to play important roles, this time as imperial sisters, rather than wives. Caligula's sisters received high distinctions and appeared as sisterly trinity in public edicts and inscriptions alongside the

emperor. Caligula had wished to have his partiality for his youngest sister Julia Drusilla sanctioned by marriage but Drusilla's death prevented this rupture with Roman moral and legal sensibilities. Gaius would have followed the precedents set by the Ptolemaic dynasty and started a development in the Roman principate which would have put it on the path of the Hellenistic monarchies. Death prevented Drusilla from mounting the throne as a sister-wife. It was her sister Julia Agrippina who was destined to restore stability and confidence to throne and empire after the unbridled sensuality of Messalina.

Messalina was the third wife of Claudius, who had emerged from the confusion occasioned by the murder of Caligula as emperor more by chance than anything else. During his reign, Messalina ruined the imperial finances by her dissolute life, surrounded the weak emperor with a circle of power-hungry freedmen, and destroyed the popularity of the imperial house by her brothel-house behaviour. Her secret betrothal to a young aristocrat, who probably was intended to occupy Claudius' throne at her side proved fatal to her. Claudius forestalled the conspiracy and condemned Messalina to death.

His young niece, Julia Agrippina, the daughter of the universally beloved Germanicus, was thought to be a virtuous woman who was nonetheless a match for her intriguing rivals. Winning and clever enough to secure the hand—or rather the throne—of her old uncle, she provided an heir to the throne with their union. Now began the reign of a clever and far-seeing woman, who helped the senate regain its authority and put an end by and large to extravagance and arbitrary rule, at any rate in the first few years of her dominance. She had the philosopher Seneca summoned back from exile and entrusted him with the education of her son, Lucius Domitius Ahenobarbus Nero, whom she caused to be adopted into the house of the Claudians and thus, with her husband's help, made into the successor to the throne. By decree of the senate, Agrippina became *Augusta*, sat at the emperor's side on public occasions and at all state affairs and dressed after the style of Hellenistic monarchs. Her position was unassailable, and she was thus able to give her undivided attention to her son's career. She succeeded in dislodging Claudius' son, Britannicus, from first place in order of succession to the throne and in tightening the family bonds by her own son's betrothal and marriage to Claudius' daughter Octavia.

Claudius died in 54 B.C., poisoned, it is said, by Agrippina, who clearly was responsible for the deaths of others whom she did not like. The real succession of events leading to the change of emperor will never be known, since even the sober writers of antiquity were blinded by prejudice. Nero became emperor and soon got tired of petticoat government. His rule was worse than any that preceded it: he dabbled in art and politics and wallowed in suspicion against all around him. The virtuous young Octavia fell victim to him, and even Poppaea Sabina, his beautiful second wife, died through his maltreatment during her second pregnancy. His awkward mother, the *optima mater* of his proclamation as Emperor, he had foully cut down in 59 B.C., after the failure of a murderous plan to have her drowned in the Gulf of Baiae by a staged shipwreck. She is said to have called out to her assassin, "Strike the body that once bore Nero."

The Flavian women never came to the forefront of the political scene in this way.

It is not until Plotina, Trajan's wife, that we come to an exemplary imperial consort. Completely under the influence of Epicureanism, she maintained a chaste dignity and integrity and influenced the succession to the imperial throne by furthering the claims of her chosen nominee, Hadrian. She even arranged his marriage for him, with the gentle Sabina, grand-niece of Trajan. Sabina led a modest and chaste life at the side of her philhellenic, travel-loving husband without excercising any notable influence on him or on the destinies of the Roman Empire.

During the rule of the dynasty of the Antonines, women again took on significant roles. Faustina the Younger, daughter of Antoninus Pius and the older Faustina, was married in 145 A.D. with pomp and ceremony to Marcus Aurelius, the adopted successor and co-regent, and on the birth of her first child received the title *Augusta*. She participated in the state affairs of the philosopher-emperor, accompanied him into war areas, and in addition to many high honours was the first Roman empress to bear the title *Mater castrorum*—mother of the camp.

With the Severi, an African-Syrian family came to the imperial throne of Rome for the first time. Fundamental social changes were leading to a new form of military monarchy. The army, the living reserve of the empire and its key power factor, put forward usurpers to the throne. Men like Maximinus Thrax and Philippus Arabs were far removed from the ancient Roman nobility and the refined late imperial culture. Septimius Severus, from Leptis Magna—an ancient town in North Africa—stood at the inception of this development. But before the tough men of the military got their hands on power de jure as well as de facto and assumed the purple toga, four Syrian women guided the Roman state.

Julia Domna, the daughter of the sun-priest Bassianus of Emesa, and the wife of Septimius Severus, introduced oriental ceremony into the veneration of the imperial house, which now approximated to an apotheosis. The empress appeared as the "new Roman Hera", as mother of the fatherland, of the senate, of the Augusti and of the camp; personified as Piety, Chastity, Fertility, as Fortuna Felix, as Harmony and Peace on coins, she was worshipped in the cult of *Virgo Caelestis*. The cultured Julia Domna influenced the intellectual trends of her time by drawing philosophers and scientists to her court and helping them to advance. But even she was to suffer the lot of an unhappy mother. After the death of Septimius Severus, her two sons, Caracalla and Geta, could not agree on a division of imperial power, and in the end Geta fell victim to his wily and brutal brother—it was said the latter murdered him in his mother's lap. The Emperor Caracalla then paid high honour to his mother and raised her to the virtual position of imperial regent. After his murder she brought on her own death by refusing to take food.

No less ambition and energy was shown by her sister Julia Maesa and her two daughters. Returning to Emesa they succeeded thanks to their considerable wealth in overthrowing Caracalla's successor, Macrinus, and in having proclaimed emperor the son of Julia Soaemias, the exceedingly handsome boy-priest of the sun, Elgabal, who however suffered from religious mania. In Rome his indomitable grandmother, Maesa, carried on the government, without however being able to prevent the growing dissatisfaction with her grandson from flaring into a revolt, which cost the life of her daughter Soaemias and her grandson Elagabal. Now it was her second grandson's turn. The mild Severus Alexander, the son of Julia Avita Mamaea, ruled after his grandmother's death with his more modest mother, who was however calamitously niggardly towards the soldiers, and with the support of the great legal expert Ulpian, who also suffered an untimely end during mutinies of soldiers. The weak emperor and his mother were not equal to the new political situation, which was becoming ever more difficult through the emergence of the new Persian empire and the revolts of the Germanic peoples, and their assassination in Germany in 235 A.D. came as no surprise. Maximius Thrax was the man who put an end to "the rule of the Syrian women" and took the imperial dignity upon his own shoulders.

With the last of the great Roman empresses, we come to the threshold of the new world of late antiquity, which was born out of the partition of the empire and the final victory of Christianity. The names of two important female rulers of the 5th and 6th centuries can stand as a postscript to our tale: Galla Placidia, the emperor's daughter who became involved in the struggle of the Goths for the Roman empire and suffered a tragic fate, and Theodora, Justinian's wife, a dancer who became Byzantine Empress.

FASHION, ORNAMENT, AND COSMETICS

"Beauty is a gift from the gods: how few can boast of it! There are too many of you who are deficient in it. Care of the person gives it charm, neglect kills its charms." *(Ovid. Ars Amat. 3, 103—5)*

In the earliest period, the Roman lady had not yet plunged into the whirlpool of fashion's follies. Like the man, she wore the simple *tunica*, a shirt-like dress, down to knees or ankles, with or without sleeves, and below it a woolly undergarment, the *subucula*, and her out-of-doors wear was a *toga*, a voluminous garment which could be wound around head and body.

There was none of the luxury and diversity which arise from the desire for individual distinction and the display of wealth. Later on, inspiration from Greece, Germania and the Orient made a great variety of forms, including indigenous and exotic elements, common wear in Rome.

Roman dress, and especially that of men, was above all the dress of social classes. Definite patterns and adornments signified the social status of the wearer. And the dress of Roman matrons differed from that of the average peasant woman, prostitute or foreign woman. A typical garment of the married lady was the *stola*, which came down to the feet, was decorated with a border, usually had half-sleeves and was gathered in at the waist by a girdle. But with the beginning of imperial times this stola was no longer fashionable, only being worn as a garment of honour by mothers with many children—*stolatae feminae*. Over the *tunnica* and *stola*, wraps were worn such as the linen *supparum*, which reached from shoulders to heel; there was in older times the *ricinum*, which was fastened on the head, or the long head-scarf or *rica*, which was worn during cult ceremonies right down to late imperial times.

Soon the Roman lady took to the lighter Greek materials; the stiff robes of thick linen and rough woollen weave gave place to soft, thin linen, cotton and silks from Greece. It was the Greek linen *chiton* with its buttoned sleeves that most took the Roman lady's fancy. The *himation*, the great cloak which enveloped the whole body, was adapted into Roman fashion as the *palla* and was worn by men and women alike; by the third century it tended to be displaced by lighter capes and a new kind of hood. Great popularity in Rome, as everywhere in the Hellenistic world, was enjoyed by the *chiton* girdled high under the bosom, and the fine, close-fitting Tarentine and Coan silk dresses, which with their attractiveness and bright colours first found favour among the venal serving maids of Aphrodite and then became the general fashion among elegant ladies. From Egypt and the Orient came new, costly textiles, threaded with gold and purple-dyed, of wool, cotton and silk.

Ovid tells us of the colourfulness of dresses:

"Shall I speak of clothes? I do not want costly trim-mings, do not want wool dyed in the blood of Tyrian snails. Since so many colours are to be had more cheaply, do not be mad and wear your whole fortune on your body! Here is the colour of the sky when it is not darkened by clouds and when the warm south wind does not fill it with rain. Comparable with you is she whom once Phrixus and Helle, so they say, rescued from Ino's wiles. This one looks like the flood, from the flood she also takes her name. Nymphs bedeck themselves with such a dress. This one is like the crocus; the dewy goddess clothes herself in crocus-garb when she harnesses her light team of horses. This one is purple like the amethyst, like the myrtles of Paphos, this one is like pale roses, that one like Thracian rabbits. Here, Amaryllis, are thy chestnuts and almond blossoms, and woollen cloths are named after wax. So many colours does the earth bear when in the warm air of spring the vine puts forth eyes, now that the winter is gone, so many colours or even more can wool drink up . . ."

(*Ovid, Ars. Amat. 3, 169 foll.*)

Egyptian materials were especially distinguished for their richness of colour and decoration. The wonderful appearance of the goddess Isis in Apuleius may have had its origin in observation of the real thing:

"The robe shimmered in many colours, was woven of fine linen, shining now splendidly white, now flashing golden yellow like saffron blossoms, now flaming rose-red. What dazzled my gaze was the cloak: deep-black, shining with dark splendour, it ran all around and came back under the right armpit to the shoulder, with a humpy fold, and one part of the material hung down in various folds. On the outer hem waved knotted fringes in a most decorative manner. All over the embroidery and upon the surface of the cloak, dotted everywhere, stars sparkled and in the middle a full moon breathed flaming fire. But everywhere where the hem of the splendid cloak ran around, there was in uninterrupted sequence an entwined series of flowers and fruits of all kinds." (*Apul. Metam. XI 20*)

Roman ladies loved ornamentation. Some of them festooned themselves—this was especially true of the less distinguished women—with fortunes in precious stones and gold ornaments. Pearls, emeralds, beryls and opals were much prized, while jewelry of glass, amber and coral was preferred by the middle class. Forty million sesterc-es was the value of the jewelry of Lollia Paulina, one of Caligula's wives. Fortunata, the wife of the parvenu Trimalchio competes with her hostess about the weight and value of her jewelry. She appeared before the guests:

"So she came in with a high yellow waist-band on, which allowed a cherry-red slip to appear under it, and twisted anklets, and white shoes embroidered with gold. She wiped her hands on a cloth which she had round her neck, took her place on the sofa, where Scintilla, Habinna's wife, was lying, kissed her as she was clap-ping her hands, and said, 'Is it really you, dear?'

Fortunata then went so far as to take the bracelets off her fat arms to exhibit them to Scintilla's admiring gaze. At last she even took off her anklets and her hair-net, which she said was eighteen carat. Trimalchio saw her, and ordered the whole lot to be brought to him. 'There', he said, 'are a woman's fetters; that is how we poor fools are plundered. She must have six pounds and a half of gold on her. I have got a bracelet myself, made out of the percentage which I owe to Mercury, that weighs not an ounce under ten pounds.' At last, for fear we should think he was lying, he ordered the scales to be brought, and had the weight carried round and tested. Scintilla was just as bad. She took off a little gold box from her neck, which she called her lucky box. Then she brought out two ear-rings, and gave them to Fortunata to look at in her turn, and said, 'Thanks to my husband's kindness, nobody has finer ones' . . ."

(M. Heseltine) (*Petronius, Trimalchio's Dinner, 67*)

Women and girls paid great attention to the care of face and hair. Ovid, the frivolous adviser to the fair sex, recommends to them the most curious folk-simples for maintaining and enhancing beauty, and who has not heard of Poppaea Sabina's baths of asses' milk? Masks of dough, tinted hair, false teeth made of ivory and wigs helped out when nature no longer responded to the ladies' wishes. Wrinkles were smeared with wax and a white make-up covering lent cheeks a tender pallor.

"You know how to paint yourself white with make-up,
and she who blooms not by nature, blooms by art.
Art teaches you to fill out the empty space between
your brows, and the cheek is covered so that it
looks as clean as a baby's skin. With fine coal-black
you shape your eyes finely, or with the yellow, which
thou, gleaming Cydnus, produceth."

(Ovid, Ars. Amat. 3, 199 foll.)

Hair styles varied from high built-up coiffures and complicated toupee of curls, which could be created with the aid of hair-pieces, to a simple parting in the middle and loosely falling strands of hair.

Ovid observed the various possibilities and described them:

"Adornment is not of one kind alone: let each one
choose for herself that which is to adorn her;
but first consult the mirror.
A simple hair-parting suits a longer face well.
That was the hair-style that Laodamia chose.
But a round face requires a low hair-knot
over the brow so that the ears cannot be seen.
This woman's curly hair flows left and right over her
shoulders, just like yours, Phoebus,
when you sing to the lyre.
But that one ties it up like Diana when, girt for the
chase, she pursues the frightened game. This one looks
well with loose hair blowing over her brow,
that one with her hair artistically disciplined and piled
up like a tower.
One tries to arrange it in the shape of a Cyllenian lyre,
while others kink their hair to look like wavelets.
But we do not count the fruits in the top of the many-
branched oak tree,
nor the bees in the meadows of Hybla
or the game on the Alps.
Nor can I recount to you the number of the various
fashions, for each new day adds something new to the
old.
Even unruly hair suits some women admirably: you
could almost believe it lies as it was combed yesterday,
but it has just this minute been combed.
Let art appear a mere accident."

(Ovid, Ars. Amat. 3, 135 foll.)

Ovid was one of the cleverest teachers the female sex ever had. He gave recipes which made it easier for any girl to make her strengths compensate for her weaknesses. The poet had, as it were, taken a peep behind the scenes and sided with the women; he did this perhaps not least out of the need to create a compensating justice for something ancient society had never known—the genuine equality of the sexes.

Thus he forged weapons for the woman, conjured up the artist-goddess of love, lent grace and charm, made beauty an applied science and reaped for it no harvest of thanks from the puritanical Augustus, who banished him to bleak Tomis at the Black Sea; but he had the undivided attention of all men and women who whether from overwhelming sensuality or in real anguish of heart turned to him as a lover of art and love.

Despite all changes in social formations Ovid has remained modern because he wrote about a fundamental human problem which has fascinated ancient and modern artists, philosophers and sociologists: woman and, for the man, how to get on with her.

The aristocratic Greek society of early times had consigned her to the house. Yet she was respected, though not so much as the Cretan woman, whose provoking dress would have been considered an outrageous offence in classical Athens.

The age of the great military successes of the Greeks over the Persians, introducing the two so-called classical centuries, was largely characterized by the absolute domination of men, despite exceptions such as Sparta; and the legal system provided no avenues to the woman for attaining independence. Every now and then there did appear lapses in the social forms by which men circumscribed the personal freedom of their partners, but these gaps did not open the domain of public activity—trade and commercial occupation to women and did not lead to the unhampered possession of private property.

One sphere of life in antiquity became, despite male dominance even in Olympus, largely a matter for women, a place of refuge for their desire for public and social activity: it was the state cults, and above all the mysteries. Just as Christian sensibility turned principally to the Mother of God in the cult of the Virgin Mary, though she at best could only be a mediator at the throne of Father and Son, the women of Greece and Rome, too, never let go entirely of the tradition of a powerful pre-Greek mother-goddess. Demeter and Kore, then later Cybele and Isis, embodying symbolically the cycle of life and nature, becoming and dying away, birth, death and repeated resurrection, were important factors in the Greek woman's existence.

In republican Rome the *mater familias*, that worthy matron, ruled as absolute mistress of the household but was largely subject to the will of her husband. For most women of the upper classes, "emancipation" meant shifting the burden—the tasks which had kept them in a state of menial dependency—onto people dependent upon them: their female servants and slaves.

Ordinary people lived without continuous matrimonial changes and testamentary disasters. The women of the small artisans and tradesmen, day-laborers and peasants had been obliged to earn the living for their families, and especially this necessity is a reason for their unfreedom. But nearly always existence for the woman of the poor classes—and especially for the female slave—meant an almost total exclusion from culture and the absence of any training of her individual and social capacities.

Date B.C.	History		Art and Architecture	Literature and Science
	Crete	*Continent*		
3000	Early Minoan I–III (2800–2000)	Late Neolithic Sesklo-Culture Dimini Culture	Appearance of painted pottery in Crete and Greece	
2500		Early Helladic (2500–1900)		
			Introduction of potter's wheel	
2000	Middle Minoan I and II	Middle Helladic (1900–1570) Immigration of Greek tribes	*Crete:* first palaces—polychrome pottery in Camares style *Greece:* simple peasant civilization, pottery with matt painting	
1500	Middle Minoan III Late Minoan I (1550–1450) Late Minoan II (1450–1400)	Late Helladic— Mycenaean. City civilization with rulers' seats	*Crete:* age of second palaces—pottery with naturalistic painting, dark on light background: then stylzed pottery in palace style	On Crete, use of Linear A writing, from which Linear B developed, in which texts especially concerned with household economy were written in Mycenaean (= Greek) language
	Late Minoan III (1400–1100)	Mycenaeans conquer Crete and spread over Aegean	*Mycene:* shaft-graves (16th century), later domed graves: fortresses with ruler's palace *(megaron)*	
1200	Migration of Greek peoples, Dorian and N. Western Greek tribes destroy Mycenaean culture—Dorian invasion Beginning of the iron age		Sub-Mycenaean style in vasepainting (continuation of tradition above all in technique) 1000–900 protogeometric pottery End of monumental architecture, murals and luxuries	Knowledge of writing is lost
900	Settlement of immigrants on level of decaying tribal order		900–850 early geometric style 850–800 austere geometric style	Development of writing from Phoenician alphabetic script
800	Emergence of aristocracy 776 Beginning of victor's list in Olympia Beginning of Greek colonization in Southern Italy and Sicily, later on Black Sea coast		800–750 fully developed geometrical style with geometrical patterns (especially meander), ornamented pottery (chief centre: Athens); first clay and bronze statuettes 750–700 late geometric style. Miniatures in bronze (horses, warriors)—oldest temples of clay brick and half-timber on stone foundation	
700	Tyranny in Corinth Messene subjugated by Sparta		700–620 early archaic style. Beginning of large sculpture and monumental architecture (esp. temples). Vases with motifs taken over from Orient (floruit of Corinthian vase-painting)	Homeric epics—Iliad and Odyssey. Hesiod, Ionian lyric: Archilochus of Paros
600	Legislation of Dracon in Athens. Solon, archon of Athens. Peisistratos tyrant of Athens.		620–570 Archaic style in sculpture— earliest life-size sculptures of youths *(kuroi)* and girls *(korai)* in free imitation of Egyptian models.	Tyrtaeus in Sparta Alcaeus of Mytilene Sappho
500	Reforms of Cleisthenes: introduction of democracy in Athens, which also becomes leading Greek state economically. Beginning of Persian Wars Ionian revolt (500–494) Marathon (490) Salamis (480)		Floruit of Attic black-figure vase-painting (painters—Clitias, Ergotismus, Exekias, Amasis). High development of late archaic sculpture Beginning of red-figure vase-painting (painter—Andocides) 500—450: early classical or pure style	Ionic natural philosophers (Thales of Miletus, Anaximander, Anaximenes). Pindar, odes to victors of athletic games Aeschylus, first great Attic tragedian

Date B.C.	History	Art and Architecture	Literature and Science
	Themistocles 1st Attic Maritime Confederacy: Athens assumes leadership Cimon Pericles Peloponnesian War (431–404) Defeat of Athens, victory of Sparta	In 5th c. floruit of Attic red-figure pottery Critius and Nesiotes, group of tyrant-slayers Myron, *Discobolus* Polygnotus of Thasos (monumental painter) Phidias, gold-ivory statues of Athena and Zeus Polyclitus, athlete with spear Classical style (450–425) Parthenon at Athens (449–432) part of democrat Pericles' building programme under direction of Phidias Painters Zeuxis and Parrhasius	Sophocles, floruit of Attic tragedy Herodotus, historian of Persian Wars Thukydides, historian of Peloponnesian War Euripides, psychological tragedies with great female roles Aristophanes, political comedy Democritus of Abdera (materialist philosopher—atomic theory) Hippocrates of Cos—founder of scientific medicine The sophists
400	War between Sparta and Persia Kings' Peace (386) 2nd Attic Maritime Confederacy. Mausolus of Halicarnassus Philipp II of Macedonia Alexander the Great subdues Persian Empire	The opulent style (425–380) Late classical style (380–325) Mausoleum of Halicarnassus (Aphrodite of Cnidus) Praxiteles ⎫ Leochares ⎪ Sculptors in Scopas ⎬ marble and bronze (furious Maenad) ⎪ Lysippus (Apoxy-omenos) ⎭	Death of Socrates (399) Plato, idealist philosopher Isocrates, orator and teacher of rhetoric Xenophon, historian
300	Struggles of Alexander's successors *(Diadochi)* Emergence of Hellenistic monarchies Celts at Delphi Foundation of Empire of Pergamum Galatian Wars of Attalus I of Pergamum	Beginning of realistic portraiture Apelles, court painter of Alexander the Great. Tanagra figures 325–230: early Hellenism Floruit of portraiture (Demosthenes), simple style 230–160: Hellenism (Group of Gauls from Pergamum—pathetic style)	Diogenes, Cynic philosopher Demosthenes, political orator Menander, chief representative of new comedy Aristotle, empirical philosopher Epicurus, founder of a school of philosophers of hedonism Zeno, founder of a school of philosophers, the Stoics Theocritus of Syracuse, idyllic lyricism Callimachus of Cyrene Archimedes of Syracuse, physicist and mathematician
200	Defeat of Macedonia Greece subjugated by Rome Destruction of Corinth (146) Pergamum subject to Rome (133)	Zeus altar of Pergamum with monumental frieze 160–100: later Hellenism (Decline in originality of Greek art, beginning of classifying period)	Polybius writes on Roman history Panaetius of Rhodes leads the school of Stoics Members of Roman senatorial oligarchy become acquainted with Greek art and philosophy Poseidonius, tutor of Pompey, Cicero and others
100	Rome extends its occupation of Hellenistic Asia Minor Last post-Alexandrine state, Egypt, subject to Rome (30)	Sitting Pugilist Portrait of Homer Increasing influence of Greek artists on maturing Roman art Laocoon group	

Date B.C.	History	Art and Architecture	Literature and Science
800	From turn of millennium, immigration of Etruscans into Central Italy 753: legendary foundation of Rome		
700	Beginning of Greek colonization in S. Italy and Sicily		
		Floruit of Etruscan goldsmith's art, etc.	
600	Floruit of Etruscan city-confederacy Etruscan monarchy in Rome	Wall-paintings in Etruscan graves Terracotta sculpture in Etruria and Rome (Vulca)	
500	Rome a republic Twelve tablets laws (451?) Rome victorious over Italic tribes	Sarcophagus sculpture Temple of Jupiter Capitolinus in Rome She-wolf Foundation and construction of important Roman temples, with aid of Greek artists	
400	Beginning of conquest of Etruria Lists of Roman officials begin Roman conquest of Veii Siege and destruction of Rome by Celts (387) Peace with Gauls, Samnites Latin Wars (304) War against Etruscan city-confederacy War with Tarentum		
300	First Punic War (264–41) Second Punic War (218–01) Syracuse and Tarentum conquered	Beginning of Roman historical painting	
200		Beginning of large-scale import of Greek works of art	
	Penetration of Eastern Mediterranian 3rd Punic War (150–146)	Engineering works in Rome, especially bridges Monument in honour of victory of Aemilius Paullus in Delphi	Ennius begins development of a Roman literature on Greek models Terence, comedies on Greek models
	Destruction of Carthage and Corinth Reforms of the Gracchi Victory over Cimbri and Teutones Sicilian Slave War	Wall-decorations, 1st period (200—80)	Cato the Elder champions conservative spirit of Rome as against Greek influence C. Lucilius, first Roman satirist
100	Dictatorship of Sulla Spartacus revolt Pompey Caesar conquers Gaul Caesar in Egypt Cleopatra	Bronze statue of Arringatore. Wall-decorations, 2nd period (80–20). From combination of central Italian and late Hellenistic elements with traditional death-masks emergence of realistic portraiture Portraits of Pompey, Cicero and Caesar Caesar's Forum	Varro, erudite and encyclopaedic writer Lucretius, didactic poet of Epicureanism Catullus, love lyrics Sallust, historian Cicero, forensic and political oratory Caesar, narrative of Gallic Wars Vergil, Aeneid, Roman epic Tibullus, Propertius, Ovid
0	Augustus (27 B.C.—14 A.D.)	Ara Pacis in honour of Augustus Portrait-statue of Augustus from Prima Porta	Livy, Roman history

Date A.D.	History	Art and Architecture	Literature and Science
	Defeat of Varus in Germany (9)	Forum of Augustus	Vitruvius, theory of architecture
	Tiberius (14—37)	Villa of Tiberius at Capri	Seneca, philosopher, Nero's tutor
	Caligula (37—41)	Imperial portraits	
	Claudius (41—54)	Wall-decorations, 3rd period	Pliny the Elder, polymath and historian
	Nero (54—68)	(20 B.C.—A.D. 40)	Juvenal, satirist
	Vespasian (69—79)	Wall-decorations, 4th period (40—79)	Plutarch, biographies of famous
	Destruction of Pompeii by eruption of	Golden House of Nero	Greeks and Romans
	Vesuvius (79)	Imperial Palaces on the Palatine	
	Titus (79—81)	Colosseum (Flavian amphitheater)	
100	Domitian (81—96)	Arch of Titus, with historical reliefs	
	Nerva (96—98)	Cancelleria reliefs	
	Adoptive Emperors:		
	Trajan (98—117), Conquest of Dacia	Forum of Trajan and market district	Suetonius, biographies of Caesars
	Hadrian (117—38)	Trajan's Column, with reliefs from	Tacitus, historian
	Antoninus Pius (138—161)	Dacian War	Pliny the Younger, Letters
	Marcus Aurelius (161—180)	Pantheon	Marcus Aurelius, Meditations
	War against Marcomanni	Hadrian's Mausoleum	Apuleius, novelist
	Commodus (180—192)	castle Saint Angelo	Pausanias, Description of Greece
		Hadrian's Villa in Tivoli (Tibur)	
		Equestrian statue of Marcus Aurelius	
		Column of Marcus Aurelius with reliefs	
		from war against Marcomanni	
200	Septimius Severus (193—211)	Triumphal arch of Septimius Severus	Church fathers:
	Caracalla (211—217)	in the forum in Rome	Origines, Clement,
	Soldier-Emperors:	Baths of Caracalla, Rome	Tertullian, Cyprian
	inc.		
	Maximinus Thrax (235—238)	Luxury sarcophagi (inc. great	Plotinus, founder of neoplatonism
	Philippus Arabs (244—249)	Ludovisian battle sarcophagus)	
		City-wall of Aurelian (against Goths)	
	Diocletian (284—305)	Baths of Diocletian, Rome	
300	Constantine (I) the Great (306—337)	Palace of Diocletian, Split	Ammianus Marcellinus
		Constantine's basilica, Rome	
		Arch of Constantine	
		Oldest Christian basilicas	

COMMENTS ON ILLUSTRATIONS

ILLUSTRATIONS IN THE TEXT

10 Mycenaean Lady in Cretan Dress with Ivory Vessel
Restored mural, height 2.27 m, from Tiryns, 13th century B.C., Athens, National Museum

11 Women as Spectators
Miniature fresco from Cnossus, Late Minoan I, about 1500 B.C., Heraklion Archaeological Museum

17 Penelope at her Loom
Skyphos by Penelope painter, height 20.5 cm, from Chiusi, about 440 B.C., Chiusi, Museo Civio, Inv. no. 1831

19 Cult Dance of Youths and Girls
From a hydria, height 53 cm, from Analatos (Attica), about 700 B.C., Athens, National Museum no. 313

21 Golden Chains
After 1400 B.C., Athens, National Museum

27 Girl in Rich Dress Spinning
Clover-leaf jug with white background by brass-founder painter, about 490 B.C., London, British Museum D 13

28/29 Women Working with Wool
Black-figured lekythos by the Amazis painter, from Vari, after middle of 6th century B.C., New York, Metropolitan Museum no. 311110

38 Hetaera Putting on Her Sandals
Nicosthenean amphora of Oltos, height 38.5 cm, from Etruria, about 520/10 B.C., former Campana collection, Paris, Louvre G 2

40 Father of Corona and her playmates
From an amphora of Euthymides, height 57.5 cm, from Vulci, about 510 B.C., Munich, Staatliche Antikensammlungen 2309

42 Aphrodite and Pan at Dice
Cover of bronze mirror, diameter 18.5 cm, about 380/70 B.C., London, British Museum 289

54 Lady in a Roman Butcher's Shop
Marble relief, 2nd century B.C., Dresden, Skulpturensammlung 418

61 Italia "Tellus Relief"
Rear of the Ara Pacis Augustae, detail, 13/9 B.C., Rome, Lungotevere in Augusta

PLATES

1 *"Parisian" Woman*
Fresco fragment from the west wing of the palace of Cnossus, Late Minoan I, about 1500 B.C., Heraklion, Archaeological Museum

2 *Women at Tree-Cult*
Gold signet ring from Cretan grave, Late Minoan II, 15th century B.C., Heraklion, Archaeological Museum

3 *Two Goddesses with Child*
Ivory group from the citadel of Mycene, height 7 cm, 15th century B.C., Athens, National Museum

4 *Goddess with Snakes*
Fayence, height 29.5 cm, from Cnossus, Late Minoan I, about 1500 B.C., Heraklion, Archaeological Museum

5 *The Bull Dance*
Fresco from east wing of palace of Cnossus, height 80 cm, Late Minoan I, about 1500 B.C., Heraklion, Archaeological Museum

6 *Woman's Head*
White marble, height 21 cm, found in Miletus near temple of Athens, about 530 B.C., Berlin, Staatliche Museen Inv. no. 1631

7 *Dancing Hetaera*
Picture on inside of a bowl by Epictetus, from Vulci, end of 6th century B.C., London, British Museum E38

8 *Statue of Woman with Pomegranate*
Marble, height 1.93 m (with plinth), found in S. Attica near Keratea, about 580/70 B.C., Berlin, Staatliche Museen Inv. no. 1800

9 *Bronze Clasp*
End of 8th century B.C., Berlin, Staatliche Museen

10 *Dionysus and Maenads*
Amphora by the Amasis painter, height 33 cm, about 540 B.C., Paris, Bibliothèque Nationale, Cabinet des Médailles

11 *Statue of Girl*
Marble, height 55.5 cm, found on the Acropolis at Athens, about 510 B.C., Athens, Acropolis Museum no. 675

12 *Hetaera and Old Man*
Picture inside bowl by Onesimus, from Vulci, about 500 B.C., London, British Museum E 44

13 *Girls in Public Well-House*
Black-figured hydria. Leagros group, height 45 cm, from Vulci, end of 6th century B.C., Berlin, Staatliche Museen Inv. no. 1908

14a) *Pair of Armbands from Sardes with Antilope Heads at Ends*
from Lydia, Perso-Grecian style, 4th century B.C., Berlin-Charlottenburg, Staatliche Museen

14b) *Chain of Golden Drops with Ram's Head*
from Eretria, 1st half of 5th century B.C., Berlin-Charlottenburg, Staatliche Museen

14c) *Neckband with Heracles Knot*
from Smyrna, 4th century B.C., Berlin-Charlottenburg, Staatliche Museen

14d) *Chain of Golden Drops and Links with Pomegranates*
from Eretria, 6th to 5th century B.C., Berlin-Charlottenburg, Staatliche Museen

15 *Statue of Woman Dedicated by Cheramyes*
Marble, height 1.67 m (with plinth), from Samos, about 560 B.C., Berlin, Staatliche Museen Inv. no. 1750

16 *Girl Standing*
Parian Marble, height 1.21 m (with plinth), from the Acropolis at Athens, about 530 B.C., Athens, Acropolis Museum no. 679

17 *Comus*
Skyphos by Brygus painter, height 19.5 cm, from Nola, about 490 B.C., Paris, Louvre G 156

18 *Girl Preparing Bath*
Picture inside bowl by Onesimus, diameter 24.2 cm, height 9 cm, from Chiusi, about 480 B.C., Brussels, Musées Royaux d'Art et d'Histoire A 889

19 *Banquet with Hetaera*
Stamnos of Smicros, height 38.5 cm, about 510 B.C., formerly Campana Collection, Brussels, Musées Royaux d'Art et d'Histoire A 717

20 *Hetaerae at Symposium*
Red-figured psycter of Euphronius, height of frieze 14 cm, about 500 B.C., Leningrad, Hermitage 644

21 *Maenad*
Amphora by the Cleophrades painter, height of amphora 56 cm, from Vulci, about 500/490 B.C., Munich, Museum antiker Kleinkunst no. 2344

22 *Alcaeus and Sappho*
Wine pitcher from circle of the Brygus painter, height 52.5 cm, from Girgenti (Sicily), about 480/470 B.C., Munich, Staatliche Antikensammlungen 2416

23a) *Geropso and Heracles*
Skyphos by the Pistoxenus painter, height 15 cm, from Caere, about 480/470 B.C., Schwerin, Staatliches Museum no. 708

23b) *Helena running from Menelaus*
Hydria by the Cleophrades painter, height 42 cm, from Nola, about 480 B.C., Naples, Museo Nazionale

24 *Throning Goddess*
Parian marble, height 1.51 m, found at Tarento, about 480 B.C., Berlin, Staatliche Museen Inv. no. 1761

25 *Drunkard and Hetaera*
Picture inside bowl by Brygus painter, diameter 32.2 cm, height 14 cm, from Vulci, about 490 B.C., Würzburg, Martin-von-Wagner Museum no. 479

26 *Girl Undressing*
Red-figured lekythos, from Gela, beginning of 5th century B.C., Syracuse, Museo Nazionale

27 *Woman Laying Garments in Trunk*
Locrian terracotta-pinax, height 26 cm, about 460 B.C., Tarento, Museo Nazionale

28 *Girl Praying*
Bronze, height 21.7 cm (with base), from Olympia (?), 460/50 B.C., Berlin, Staatliche Museen Inv. no. 30082

29 *Women Preparing Wool*
Bowl by Duris, diameter 33 cm, from Vulci, after 480 B.C., Berlin-Charlottenburg, Staatliche Museen no. 2289

30 *Three Girls at Wash Basin*
Stamnos, from Vulci, group by Polygnotus, about middle of 5th century B.C., Munich, Museum antiker Kleinkunst 2411

31 *Birth of Aphrodite*
Front view of Ludovisian throne, marble, height originally 1.07 m, length 1.43 m, about 460 B.C., Rome, Museo Nazionale Romano

32 *Mother and Child in Small Chair*
Picture inside bowl by Sotades, diameter 12.7 cm, about middle of 5th century B.C., Brussels, Musées Royaux Cinquanténaire Inv. no. 890

33 *Two Women and Child*
Lekythos with white background by Achilles painter, height 36.8 cm, from Picrodaphai in Attica, middle of 5th century B.C., Berlin-Charlottenburg, Staatliche Museen F. 2443

34a) *Head of Arethusa*
Syracusan coin, about 450 B.C., private collection

34b) *Scythian Comb*
Gold, height 12.5 cm, about 430/20 B.C., Leningrad, Hermitage

35 *Aphrodite in Peplos*
Bronze stand mirror from Megara, height 37.9 cm, about 450 B.C., Dresden, Albertinum Inv. ZV 807

36 *Female Lapith*
Marble, from west pediment of temple of Zeus, Olympia, about 460 B.C., Olympia, Museum

37 *Female Playing Flute*
Left-hand side of the Ludovisian throne, height 83.5 cm, length 72 cm, about 460 B.C., Rome, Museo Nazionale Romano

38 *Woman Spinning*
Red-figured tripod-pyxis, in the style of the late works of the Panaitius painter, beginning of 5th century B.C., Athens, National Museum 1584

39 *Dead Man Lying in*
Lutrophorus by the Cleophrades painter, height 81 cm, from Attica, about 480 B.C., Paris, Louvre CA 453

40 *Youthful Athena*
Relief dedicated to goddess, marble, height 54 cm, from the Acropolis, to the south of the Parthenon, about 460 B.C., Athens, Acropolis Museum no. 695

41 *Women with Offertory Vessels on the Way to Grave*
Lekythos with white background by Achilles painter, from Eretria, about 460 B.C., Athens, National Museum

42 *Woman Sacrificing at the Scira*
Red-figured lekythos, group from Palermo 16, 2nd half of 5th century B.C., Athens, National Museum no. 1695

43 *Wounded Amazon,*
Marble, Roman copy, height 1.82 m, about 430 B.C., Berlin, Staatliche Museen Inv. no. 7

44 *Girl at Graveside*
Stele Giustiniani, marble, height 1.43 m, about 460 B.C., Berlin, Staatliche Museen Inv. no. 1482

45 *Two Women at Graveside*
Lekythos with white background by the "Women" painter, height 39 cm, from Eretria in Euboea, about 430/20 B.C., Athens, National Museum no. 1956

46 *Relief on Grave of Hegeso*
Marble, height 1.49 m, end of 5th century B.C., Athens, National Museum 3624

47 *Dying Niobid*
Marble, height 1.49 m, about 440 B.C., Rome, Museo Nazionale Romano

48 *Warrior's Farewell*
Stamnos by Cleophon painter, height 44 cm, from Vulci, about 430 B.C., Munich, Museum antiker Kleinkunst no. 2415

49 *Scene at Cult of the Dead*
Lekythos with white background of the Athens painter 1329, height 42 cm, from Eretria, about 460 B.C., Brussels, Musées Royaux d'Art et d'Histoire A 1019

50 *Women with Wedding Gifts*
Lebes of the Marsyas painter, height 46 cm, from Kertch (Pantikapeion), about 335 B.C., Leningrad, Hermitage 15592

51a) *Helena's Toilette*
Bowl by the Berlin painter 2536, height 13.5 cm, from Nola, about 430 B.C., Berlin-Charlottenburg, Staatliche Museen F 2536

51b) *Muses Playing*
Italiot volute crater-cup by the Sisyphus painter, height of frieze 24.3 cm, from Ruvo, about 420 B.C., Munich, Museum antiker Kleinkunst 3268

52 *Swing Festival*
Red-figured skyphos by the Penelope painter, height 20 cm, about 440 B.C., Berlin, Staatliche Museen no. 2589

53 *Women Baking a Wedding-cake*
Red-figured lekane by the Eleusinian painter, from Kertch, about 400 B.C., Leningrad, Hermitage 1791

54a) *Women at Washing Festival*
Red-figured wine-jar by the Meidias painter, from Athens, end of 5th century B.C., New York, Metropolitan Museum of Art 75.2.11

54b) and 55 Epinetron by the Eretria Painter
Length 29 cm, from Eretria, about 420 B.C., Athens, National Museum

56 Dancer with Castanettes
Terracotta, height 18.3 cm, from Athens, about 350 B.C., Berlin, Staatliche Museen T.C. 6822

57 Dionysian Festival
Red-figured stamnos by Dinos painter, height 49 cm, from Nocera de' Pagani (Campania), about 420 B.C., Naples, Museo Nazionale 2419

58 Lovers
Wine-jar by the Shuvalov painter, height 19 cm, from Locri, about 430/20 B.C., Berlin-Charlottenburg, Staatliche Museen F 2414

59 Symposium
Campanian bell-crater (cup) from Cumae, C A painter, 3rd quarter of 4th century B.C., Naples, Museo Nazionale Inv. 85873

60 The "Dew-Sisters", from Eastern Pediment of Parthenon, Athens
Marble, height 1 m, about 437/32 B.C., London, British Museum

61 Girls playing at Knucklebones
Painting on marble, Roman copy, height 42 cm, from Herculaneum, original—end of 5th century B.C., Naples, Museo Nazionale

62 Dancer with Tambourine
Terracotta, height 19.5 cm, from S. Russia, middle of 4th century B.C., Berlin, Staatliche Museen T.C. 8821

63 Female Acrobat
Apulian pelike from Naples, height 22 cm, 3rd century B.C., Berlin, Staatliche Museen Inv. 3444

64 Maenad
Marble, Roman copy, height 45 cm, about 350 B.C., Dresden, Staatliche Kunstsammlungen Inv. no. 133

65 Washing Hair
Red-figured pelike, Athens painter 1472, about 340 B.C., Athens, National Museum 1472

66 Serving Maid at Sacrifice "Antium girl"
Parian marble, Roman copy, height 1.70 m, found in Roman villa of imperial period at Antium (Anzio), about 240 B.C., Rome, Museo Nazionale Romano

67 Aphrodite Crouching
Marble, Roman copy, height 1.02 m, from the Villa Hadriana near Tivoli, about 250 B.C., Rome, Museo Nazionale Romano Inv. no. 557

68 Dancer
Terracotta, height 22 cm, from Megara, Hellenistic, Berlin, Staatliche Museen Inv. F 2919 (T.C. 7092)

69 Terracotta Statuette of Young Woman
Height 24 cm, from Tanagra, end of 4th century B.C., Berlin, Staatliche Museen T.C. 7674

70 Niobe and Her Youngest Daughter
Marble, Roman copy, height 2.27 m, about 280 B.C., Florence, Uffizi

71 Statue of Nicoclea, Priestess of Demeter
Marble, height 1.57 m, found in Demeter sanctuary of Cnidus, after middle of 3rd century B.C., London, British Museum

72 Diadem of Blossoms
Gold filigree, diameter 15 cm, from Canosa, 3rd century B.C., Tarento, Museo Nazionale Inv. no. 22437

73 Statue of Woman "Little Woman of Herculaneum"
Marble, Roman copy, height 1.70 m, from Herculaneum, about 330 B.C., Dresden, Staatliche Kunstsammlungen Inv. no. 326

74 Nurse and Child
Terracotta, height 26.8 cm, from Myrina, about 100 B.C., Berlin, Staatliche Museen T.C. 7946

75 Girl Playing at Knucklebones,
Marble, Roman copy, height 70 cm, 2nd half of 3rd century B.C., Berlin, Staatliche Museen Inv. no. 494

76 Women at Cult of Dead
Amphora with lid, height 56 cm, from Centuripe, 3rd century B.C., Catania, Instituto di Archeologia dell'Università

77 Venus of Milo
Marble, height 2.04 m, found on island of Melos, 2nd quarter of 2nd century B.C., Paris, Louvre no. 399/400

78 Aphrodite and Pan
Marble, height 1.32 m, from Delos, about 100 B.C., Athens, National Museum 3335

79 Drunken Old Woman
Marble, Roman copy, height 92 cm, last third of 3rd century B.C., Munich, Glyptothek no. 467

80 Fighting Goddess
North frieze of Pergamum altar, marble, height 2.30 m, 180–160 B.C., Berlin, Staatliche Museen

81 Aphrodite Statuette
Terracotta, height 37.6 cm, from Asia Minor after middle of 2nd century B.C., (former Heyl collection), Berlin, Staatliche Museen Inv. no. 31272

82/83 Greek Goddesses

82 a) Athena
From west pediment of temple of Aphaia on Aegina, about 510 B.C., Munich, Glyptothek

82 b) Hera Unveiling before Zeus
Metope from temple of Hera in Selinunt, about 450 B.C., Palermo, Museo Nazionale

82 c) Artemis
East frieze of Parthenon, about 430 B.C., Athens, Acropolis Museum

82 d) Aphrodite of Cnidos
Marble, Roman copy, original by Praxiteles, height 2.05 m, about 350 B.C., Rome, Vatican Museum

BIBLIOGRAPHY

1 Abrahams, E.; Lady Evans: *Ancient Greek dress*. A new illustrated edition. Chicago 1964

2 Adcock, F. E.: *Women in Roman Life and Letters. Greece and Rome* XIV, 1945, 1 foll.

3 Assa, J.: *Les grandes dames romaines*. Paris 1958
La donna nell'antica Roma. Milano 1960

4 d'Avino, M.: *The woman of Pompeii*. Naples 1967

5 Baldson, J. P. V. D.: *Women in Imperial Rome*. History today 1, 1960, 24 foll.

6 Beauvoir, Simone de: *Das andere Geschlecht. Eine Deutung der Frau*. Hamburg 1960

7 Bieber, M.: *Entwicklungsgeschichte der griechischen Tracht*. Berlin 1967, 2nd ed.

8 Bieber-Lux, Dora: *Die Frau in der griechischen Sage und Geschichte*. Berlin 1927

9 Birt, Th.: *Die Cynthia des Properz*. Leipzig 1922;
Frauen der Antike. Leipzig 1932

10 Boer, W. Den: *Eros en Amor, Man en Vrouw in Griekenland en Rome*. The Hague 1962

11 Brindesi, F.: *La famiglia attica, Il matrimonio e l'adozione*. Biblioteca di Cultura 66. Florence 1961

12 Bromberg, A. R.: *Concordia. Studies in Roman marriage under the Empire*. Harvard Studies. In: Clacssial Philology 66. 1962, 249 foll.

13 Bruns, J.: *Frauenemancipation in Athen. Ein Beitrag zur attischen Kulturgeschichte des fünften und vierten Jahrhunderts*. Kiel 1900

14 Buddenhagen, F.: *Περὶ γάμου*. Diss. Basel 1919

15 Carcopino, J.: *La vita quotidiana a Roma all'apogeo dell-Impero*. Bari 1967, 380 p.

16 Conzelmann, H.: *Korinth und die Mädchen der Aphrodite. Zur Religionsgeschichte der Stadt Korinth*. Göttingen 1967

17 Csillag, P.: *Das Eherecht des augusteischen Zeitalters*. Klio 50 (1968) 111—138

18 Daniel, W. B. Mc.: *Roman private life and its survivals*. London 1925

19 Demargne, P.: *Die Geburt der griechischen Kunst*. Munich 1965

20 Deubner, L.: *Attische Feste*. Berlin 1956

21 Duke, T. T.: *Women and Pygmies in the Roman Arena*. The Classical Journal 50, 1955, 223 foll.

22 Durry, M.: *Sur le mariage romain*. Gymnasium 63, 1956, 187 foll.

23 Eglinton, J. Z.: *Griechische Liebe*. Translated by A. Y. Millrath. Hamburg 1967

24 Erdmann, W.: *Die Ehe im alten Griechenland*. Münchener Beiträge zur Papyrusforschung und antiken Rechtsgeschichte. No. 20. Munich 1934.

25 Etienne, R.: *La vie quotidienne à Pompéi*. Paris 1966

26 Eydoux, H. P.: *Les grandes dames de l'archéologie*. Paris 1964

27 Ferrero, G.: *Die Frauen der Cäsaren*. Stuttgart 1921, 3rd ed.

28 Flacelière, R.: *Love in ancient Greece*. New York 1962

29 Förtsch, Barbara: *Die politische Rolle der Frau in der römischen Republik.* Würzburger Studien zur Altertumswissenschaft, No. 5. Stuttgart 1935

30 Friedländer, L.: *Sittengeschichte Roms.* Cologne 1957, 2nd ed.

31 Gaudemet, I.: *Les transformations de la vie familiale au bas empire et l'influence du christianisme.* Romanitas. 4, 1962, 58 foll.

32 Gomme, A. W.: *The Position of Women in Athen in the fifth and fourth Centuries.* Classical Philology XX, 1925, No. 1, 1 foll.

33 Grejs, E. (Kasakewitsch): *O konkubinate v Afinach klassitscheskogo perioda.* Vestnik Drevnej Istorii 1968, I. 28—52

34 Grimal, P.: *La vie à Rome dans l'Antiquité.* Paris 1953

35 Helm, R.: *Römisches Alltagsleben im 1. und 2. Jahrhundert nach Martial und Juvenal.* Zurich 1963

36 Henne am Rhyn, O.: *Die Frau in der Kulturgeschichte.* Berlin 1892, 2nd ed.

37 Herfst, P.: *Le travail de la femme dans la Grèce ancienne.* Diss., Utrecht 1922.

38 Herrmann, Claudine: *Le rôle judiciaire et politique des femmes sous la République romaine.* Collection Latomus LXVIII. Brussels/Berchem 1964

39 Herrmann, J.: *Die Ammenverträge in den gräko-ägyptischen Papyri.* Zeitschrift der Savigny-Stiftung für Rechtsgeschichte, 76. Weimar 1959, 490 foll.

40 Hirvonen, K.: *Matriarchal survivals and certain trends in Homer's female characters.* Helsinki 1968

41 Hooper F. A.: *Greek realities. Life and thought in ancient Greece.* New York 1967

42 Hope, Th.: *Costumes of the Greeks and Romans* (Repr.). London/New York 1962

43 Jax, K.: *Der Frauentypus der römischen Dichtung.* Innsbruck 1938. *Die weibliche Schönheit in der griechischen Dichtung.* Innsbruck 1933

44 Jenzer, A.: *Wandlungen in der Auffassung der Frau im ionischen Epos und in der attischen Tragödie bis auf Sophokles.* Diss. Basle 1933

45 Kahrstedt, U.: *Kulturgeschichte der römischen Kaiserzeit.* Munich 1944

46 Kakridis, J. Th.: *The role of the woman in the Iliad.* Eranos LIV, 1956, 21 foll.

47 Kaser, M.: *Das Römische Privatrecht.* I Munich 1955: II Munich 1959. Handbuch der Altertumswissenschaft. 3rd part, vol. III, chapter 2

48 Klepper, E.: *Das Büchlein der Gewandung. Von der Frühzeit bis zum Ausgang der Antike.* Berlin 1963

49 Königer, H.: *Gestalt und Welt der Frau bei Tacitus.* Diss. Erlangen/Nuremberg 1966

50 Kornemann, E.: *Die Stellung der Frau in der vorgriechischen Mittelmeerkultur.* Heidelberg 1927. *Große Frauen des Altertums.* Wiesbaden 1952

51 Laccy, W. K.: *The family in classical Greece.* London 1968

52 La Femme: *Recueils de la Societé Jean Bodin XI.* Brussels 1959

53 Latte, K.: *Römische Religionsgeschichte.* Handbuch der Altertumswissenschaft. 5th sect., part 4, Munich 1960

54 Lefébure, Ch.: *Le Mariage et le divorce à travers l'histoire romaine.* In: Nouvelle Revue historique du Droit français et étranger, XLII, 120 foll.

55 Leipoldt, J.: *Die Frau in der antiken Welt und im Urchristentum.* Leipzig 1965, 3rd ed.

56 Licht, H.: *Sittengeschichte Griechenlands.* Stuttgart 1959

57 *Marinatos, S.: Kreta und das mykenische Hellas.* Munich 1959

58 Marquardt, J.: *Römische Staatsverwaltung* III. Darmstadt 1957. 3rd ed. *Das Privatleben der Römer* I. u. II. Darmstadt 1964, reprint 1886, 2nd ed.

59 Nilsson, M. P.: *Die Grundlagen des spartanischen Lebens.* Klio 12, 1912, 308 foll.

60 Paoli, U. E.: *Das Leben im alten Rom.* Bern 1948

61 *Paulys Realencyclopädie der Classischen Altertumswissenschaft,* edited by G. Wissowa, vol. 1, 1894 foll.

62 Pernice, E.: *Griechisches und römisches Privatleben.* In: Einleitung in die Altertumswissenschaft II, 1st part, Leipzig/Berlin 1922

63 Pfister, K.: *Die Frauen der Cäsaren.* Berlin/Zurich/Vienna 1951

64 Rademacher, L.: *Die Stellung der Frau innerhalb der griechischen Kultur.* Mitteilungen des Vereins der Freunde des humanistischen Gymnasiums 27, 1929, 6 foll.

65 Rawson, B.: *Family life among the lower classes at Rome in the first two centuries of the Empire.* Classical Philology 61, 1966, 71 foll.

66 *Reallexikon für Antike und Christentum.* Cf. vol. III, "Dirne", 1154 foll. (H. Herter); cf. IV "Ehe", 650 foll. (A. Oepke)

67 Roveri, A.: *La vita familiare nella Grecia antica.* Enciclopedia classica 3, 1959, 379 foll.

68 Schadewaldt, W.: *Sappho. Welt und Dichtung. Dasein in der Liebe.* Potsdam 1951

69 Schichtegroll, C. F. v.: *Liebesleben im Klassischen Altertum.* Leipzig (no year)

70 Seltman, Ch.: *The statues of women in Athens.* Greece and Rome. Ser. 2, Nos. 1. 2., 1954/55, 119 foll. *Women in Antiquity.* London 1956 *Geliebte der Götter. Eine Kulturgeschichte der Frau im Altertum.* Stuttgart 1958

71 Seyfarth, W.: *Ehen zwischen freien Frauen und Sklaven. Ein Beitrag zur Frage der Entwicklung der Beziehungen zwischen den Freien und der Sklavenklasse in den ersten sechs Jahrhunderten u. Z.* Byzantinistische Beiträge. Berlin 1964, 41 foll.

72 Shear, T. L.: *Koisyra, Three women of Athens.* Phoenix (Toronto) 17, 1963, 99 foll.

73 Sonnet-Altenburg, H.: *Hetären — Mütter — Amazonen. Frauencharaktere aus der antiken Welt.* Heidenheim 1963

74 Stahr, A.: *Römische Kaiserfrauen.* Berlin 1880

75 Vogt, J.: *Von der Gleichwertigkeit der Geschlechter in der bür-
gerlichen Gesellschaft der Griechen*. Abhandlung der Akade-
mie der Wissenschaften und der Literatur. Mainz, 1960,
No. 2, 213 foll.

76 Voigt, M.: *Die römischen Altertümer, 3. Privataltertümer und
Kulturgeschichte*. Handbuch der klassischen Altertumswissenschaft vol. IV, section 2, 272 foll. Munich 1893,
2nd ed.

77 Williams, G.: *Some aspects of Roman marriage ceremonies and
ideals*. The Journal of Roman Studies 48, 1958, 16 foll.

78 Wissowa, G.: *Religion und Kultur der Römer*. Handbuch der
Klassischen Altertumswissenschaft. vol. V, sect. 4, Munich 1912, 2nd ed.

79 Wolf, G.: *Geschichte der Frisur in allen Zeiten*. Darmstadt
1952

SOURCES OF ILLUSTRATIONS

Athens, National Museum: 38, 41, 42, 54, 55b, 65, 78.
Berlin-Charlottenburg, Stiftung Preußischer Kulturbesitz,
Staatliche Museen, Antikenabteilung: 14a–d, 29, 33, 51a,
58.
Berlin, Staatliche Museen, Antikensammlung: 6, 8, 9, 13,
15, 24, 28, 43, 44, 52, 56, 62, 63, 68, 69, 74, 75, 80, 81, 83c,
86, 87, 94a–c, 95c, d, f.
Brunswick, Georg Westermann Verlag: 109.
Cinisello Balsamo (Milan), Amilcare Pizzi S.p.A., Arti Gra-
fiche: 72, 101a.
Dresden, Staatliche Kunstsammlungen: 64, 73, 95a.
Florence, Fratelli Alinari: 26, 70, 85, 88–92, 94d, e, 97, 106,
110, 111.
Florence, SCALA Instituto Fotografico Editoriale: Title
picture, 1, 61, 84, 93, 96, 98, 99, 102, 103, 105a, b, 108, 112.
Geneva, Musée d'Art et d'Histoire: 101b.
Leningrad, Hermitage: 20, 34b, 50, 53, 107.
London, British Museum: 7.
Meißen, Wilfried Grahl: 35.
Munich, Hirmer-Fotoarchiv: 2–5, 10, 11, 12, 16-19, 21, 22,
23b, 25, 27, 31, 32, 34a, 36, 37, 39, 40, 45-49, 57, 60, 66,
67, 71, 76, 77, 82a–d, 83a, b.
Munich, Staatliche Antikensammlungen: 30, 51b, 79, 95e.
Munich, Verlag F. Bruckmann: 83d.
Naples, Museo Nazionale: 59.
New York, Metropolitan Museum of Art: 55a.
Rome, Soprintendenza alle Antichità: 94f, 95b.
Schwerin, Klaus Nitsche: 23a.
Trier, Rheinisches Landesmuseum: 100.
Vienna, Kunsthistorisches Museum: 104.

ILLUSTRATIONS

"Parisian" woman, fresco. Stark contrasts of black hair and made-up eye, full red mouth and delicate white skin are the attractive features of this Minoan picture, in which archaeologists have thought they had discovered the particular saucy charm of the Frenchwoman of her time.

"Parisian" woman, fresco. Stark contrasts of black hair and made-up eye, full red mouth and delicate white skin are the attractive features of this Minoan picture, in which archaeologists have thought they had discovered the particular saucy charm of the Frenchwoman of her time.

Woman at tree-cult, Minoan signet-ring. Cretan women in long flounced skirt and with upper part of body exposed carry out a ritual ceremony in the open air.

3

Goddess with snakes, fayence. Below a short sleeved bodice, laced in and fastened by a wide girdle, the goddess wears a skirt with seven flounces, with an apron over her lap. Upon her head she wears a flat, ornamented turban.

The bull dance, fresco. Cretan girls also participated in the perilous bull-dance. Clad in an apron only, they faced the bull, swung themselves up on its horns and flew over its back in a hazardous salto mortale.

Statue of woman with pomegranate. Over the chiton with its meander pattern the goddess (Aphrodite or Persephone) wears a carefully folded cape with tassels on the hem. A polos on the head, rich jewelry and high-toed sandals underline the noble rank of the person represented.

Bronze clasp. This piece of jewelry used as a clasp for the garment shows figures and an ornament in fine chasing.

Dionysus and Maenads, from an Attic amphora. Two girls, their arms tightly intertwined, devotees of the wine-god, meet their master, Dionysus. Trailing ivy, fawn and leopard-skin point to the cult of Dionysus.

Statue of girl by sculptor of Ionian islands. An originally dark-blue chiton and a bright, coloured cape envelop the graceful girl. In her hair she wears a diadem of metal.

Hetaera and old man, painting inside bowl. The hetaera is loosening her girdle, which holds together the broad, finely pleated chiton, in order to lie down with her ageing lover. On her head she wears a coloured, pointed hood. She has laid her stringed instrument aside.

Girls in public well-house, from a black-figured hydria. They wear the long chiton decorated with stars and dots, and over it a short cape in many folds or a long cloak. The hair falls down over the back from a ribbon fixed in the curls; a carrying pad allows the hydria to be held firmly on the head. The girls hold blossoms in their hands. Fawns and trailing creepers together with the portico and the lion's head indicate a ceremonial occasion in the open air.

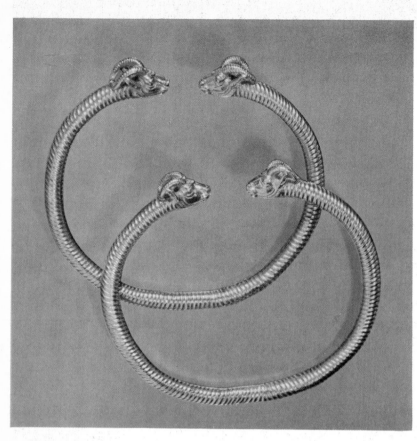

Pair of armbands from Sardes with antilope heads at ends.

Chain of golden drops with ram's head as central pendant.

Neckband with Heracles knot of plaited gold wire, with pendants.

Chain of golden drops and intermediate links in the form of pomegranates.

Statue of woman, from Samos, dedicated by Cheramyes. Over a finely pleated, girdled chiton the woman wears a cloak, which hangs down on the right knee-length in two broad lappets. A folded veil covers head, back and left hip. The hare is a gift dedicated to her; she is probably meant to be Aphrodite, for whom the gift is intended.

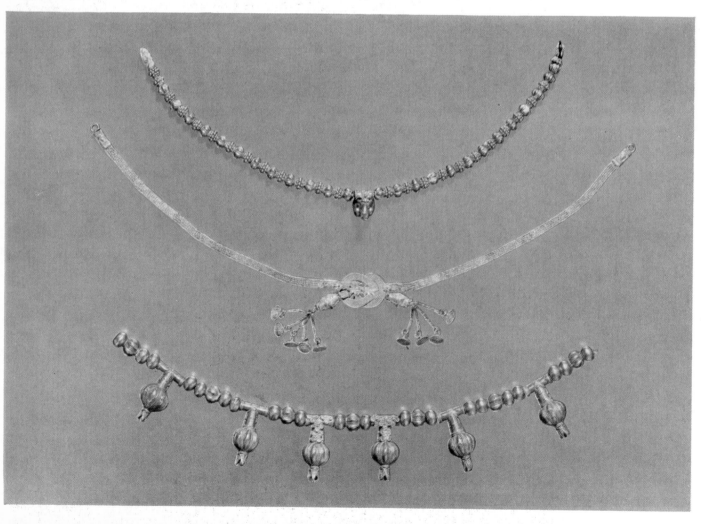

Girl standing. This long-haired Athenian girl appears before us in the Dorian peplos, under which she wears a thin chiton.

Comus (revel), from an Attic drinking cup. Two richly dressed hetaerae move homewards with their lovers from a banquet. The men's uncertain gait is an indication of their bibulous high spirits.

Girl preparing bath, painting inside Attic bowl. A short-haired girl carries water in a bronze vessel; a washbowl stands before her.

Banquet with hetaera, from an Attic stamnos. The hetaera Chloro (the name is inscribed on the jar) twines a ribbon round her hair. Her chiton enhances the charm of her body.

Hetaerae at symposium, from an Attic psycter (= wine-cooler). The names of the drinkers are given. Sekline plays the flute; Palaesto—the wrestler—drinks out of a cantharos; Smicra tosses the lees of her drinking cup in an oracular love-game.

Maenad, from an Attic amphora. The frenzied maenad wears an ivy chaplet in her hair and carries on her shoulders the thyrsus, symbol of the god, Dionysus. She has thrown a leopard-skin over her chiton.

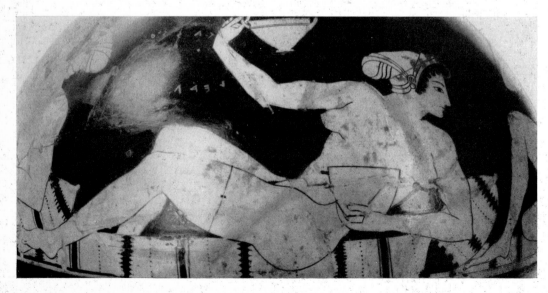

*Alcaeus and Sappho, from an Attic wine-pitcher. Sappho, in long
chiton and cloak, in her hair a ribbon and diadem, listens to Alcaeus
singing to the accompaniment of a lyre.*

Geropso and Heracles, from an Attic skyphos. Heracles is being taken by a faithful old nurse to his music lesson.

Helena running from Menelaus, from an Attic hydria. In order to escape from her revenge-seeking husband, the naked Helena embraces the statue of the goddess Athena. Then—conquered by her beauty—his wrath abates and he accepts her again as his wife.

Throning goddess, from Tarento. The goddess of the underworld, Persephone, sits in her rich, late archaic dress upon an artistically carved and upholstered throne. She is dressed in a thin, pleated chiton with a round neckline. Over this she wears a cape buttoned up over the right arm and falling in two symmetrical points over the knees. The goddess has thrown a shawl over back and shoulders; its points hanging down under the arms of the throne. The beautiful hair is gathered under a hood and held back over the brow by a diadem.

Drunkard and hetaera, interior painting of an Attic bowl. A short-haired hetaera, with a chaplet of vine leaves, carefully tends a drunken reveller.

25

Girl undressing for the bath, from a red-figured lekythos. The Greek woman knew that water was the best beauty treatment for the skin. She washed in a bowl. For this purpose she fetched water in large pitchers.

Woman laying garments in a trunk, terracotta pinax. The garment is carefully kept in a chest. In the background in relief are a basket, a mirror, a lekythos and a beaker hanging up.

26

Girl praying. The girl is dressed in a peplos, the upper third of which, thrown back, is worn as an apoptygma (fold-back cape). Originally she held some object in her hand. She has also been thought to be a girl spinning wool.

Women preparing wool, from an Attic bowl. By twisting over the naked lower leg the wool is worked into a thread and thus prepared for spinning. The woman supports her foot on a stand. Two baskets contain the material to be processed.

Three girls at wash basin. They are doing their personal toilet.

Birth of Aphrodite. Front view of the "Ludovisian" throne. Aphrodite rises up from the watery depths and is helped and received by two women. She appears as "Anadyomene"—rising up from the waters. According to one version of the myth she was born from the foam of the sea.

Mother and child, picture inside bowl. A safe baby-chair prevents accidents.

ΔΡΟΜΙ[Π]...[Π]ΟΣ
ΚΑΛΟΣ   ...ΛΕΙΔΟ
ΔΡΟΜΟΚΛ

Two women and child, from an Attic lekythos. Affectionate gesture of human attachment and at the same time of inexorable parting in death; a young mother receives her child for the last time.

Head of spring-nymph Arethusa on a Syracusan coin. The hair, parted in the middle, is bound up with a narrow ribbon and tied in waves.

Scythian gold comb, decorated with battle-scenes.

Stand-mirror. Aphrodite in Dorian peplos as support. The mirror was part of the toilette equipment of every rich civic woman. Its surface was polished so that it shone, and edges and reverse side ornamented.

Female Lapith. The young wife is in danger of being carried off by drunken Centaurs at her wedding-feast. Her bridegroom Pirithous and the other Lapiths (Greeks) rescue her with Apollo's help.

Left side of the "Ludovisian" throne. A naked hetaera, servant of the goddess of love, plays upon the double flute.

Woman spinning. A richly-dressed woman is busy preparing wool. The representation is to be found on an Attic box, which was used for keeping jewelry and toilette articles in.

Dead man lying in, from an Attic black urn. Several women tend a youthful corpse. They raise their arms in lamentation and have their hair cut short as a sign of mourning. Mourning women carry a black urn to the grave.

39

Youthful Athena, dedicatory relief. A girlish Athena, clad in a peplos, leans meditatively on a spear.

Women with offertory vessels on the way to grave. Lekythos from Eretria.

Sacrifice to Scira, from an Attic lekythos. At the festival of Scira a woman sacrifices a young pig to the goddesses of the underworld, Demeter and Kore. In the sacrificial basket she carries loaves in the shape of snakes and phalluses, which are thrown into the Megara (pits) together with the pig.

43

Girl at graveside, relief on a grave stele. A girl in an ungirdled peplos open at one side takes a ribbon from a box to decorate the pillar on a grave.

Two women at a graveside, from a white Attic lekythos. A mourning woman sits upon the steps of a grave. Behind her a servant girl dressed in a short chiton, approaches with a basket of fruit.

Relief on grave of Hegeso. A moment out of everyday life of the beautiful Hegeso. Wrapped in chiton and cloak, she sits in an armchair and together with her serving-maid holds a jewel casket, from which she takes a necklace, which was originally painted on the stele.

Dying Niobid. The daughter of Niobe collapses, struck in the back by an arrow from Artemis. She pays with her life for her mother's inordinate pride in her twelve children.

Warrior's farewell, from an Attic stamnos. A fully armed warrior lifts up his bowl for a farewell drink. Filled with sadness the young wife in her peplos lowers her head.

Scene at cult of the dead, from an Attic white lekythos. The young woman with the long, curly hair holds a taenia in her hands. A female slave in a black gown hands her an ornamented casket. Toilet articles, a mirror and a lekythos, hang from the wall.

48

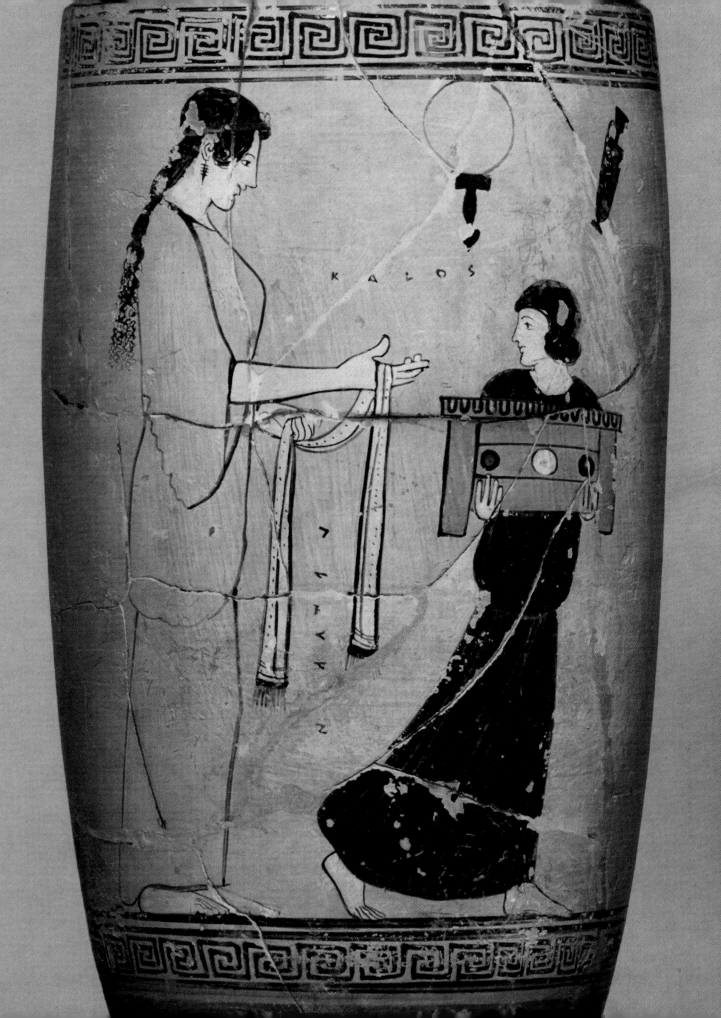

Women with wedding gifts, from a lebes. Epaulia—the presentations to the newlyweds on the morning of their wedding. The beautiful women, clad in chiton and cloak, bring an Eros statuette, a lutrophora (black urn), several caskets and a pile of bedclothes as wedding presents.

Helena's toilette. She eloped from her husband Menelaus with Paris, son of the Trojan king and thus became the occasion of the Trojan War.

Muses playing, from an Italiot volute crater. The Muses clad in thin chitons have gathered together for a concert in a hall with their zither, harp, tortoise-lyre and flutes.

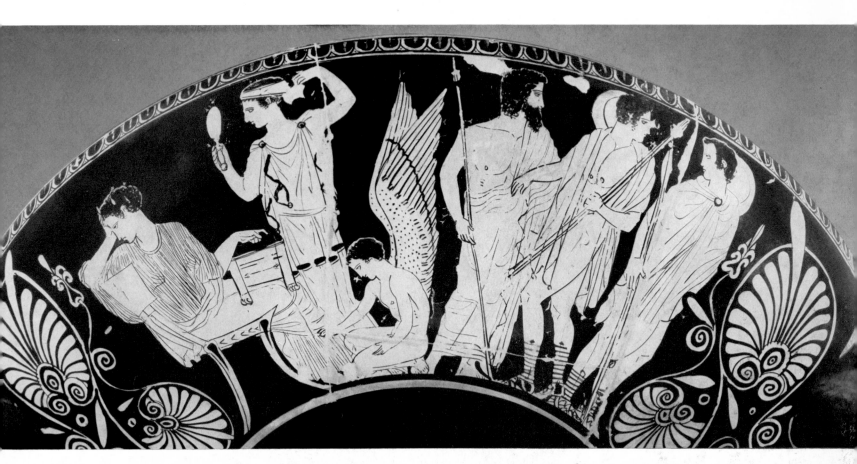

Swing festival, skyphos. A satyr swings a young Athenian woman. The swing festival of Aeora was celebrated on the third day of the Anthesteria, sacred to Dionysus, in spring. The swing consists of a stool suspended on ropes. The words refer to the girl: "You are beautiful, Anthea."

Women at the washing festival, from an Attic wine-jar. Two women are engaged in sprinkling their colourfully woven clothes with scent for the feast of Chosa. For this they use a small lekythos. The clothes are piled up on a stool suspended by ropes.

The distaff is held conveniently near to the spinning woman's thigh. It served to smooth down the wool in order to shape the thread. As decoration, scenes about Alcestis as a bride are used.

Dancer with castanettes, terracotta. The dancer in calf-length, high-girdled chiton whirls to the rhythm of her rattling castanettes.

Dionysian festival, from an Attic stamnos. Maenads have gathered for the cult celebration before the clothed Herme of the wine-god Dionysus. The picture suggests the Attic Lenaea, a Dionysian festival of an orgiastic character.

Lovers, wine-jar from Locri. In Greek vase-paintings, as here, erotic scenes may be frequently encountered.

Symposium, from a Campanian bell-crater. Two hetaerae and three youths have gathered for a drinking bout. One girl plays the flute while the other has settled down in tender intimacy on the couch of her lover. A little servant brings food and drink.

The "Dew-Sisters" from the eastern pediment of Parthenon, Athens. The three voluptuous women have been identified as Leto, Dione and Aphrodite. They look on at the birth of Athene, represented in the centre of the pediment.

Girls playing at knucklebones. Painting on marble. The painting bears the signature of Alexander of Athens. He painted it after an original of classical times. The legends place the young women in the realm of myth. The later worst enemies, Leto and Niobe, are here being reconciled by Phoebe.

Dancer with tambourine. A young girl beats the tambourine in time to the dance.

Female acrobat on an Apulian pelike (= pitcher) holds bow and arrow with her feet.

63

Maenad. The half-life size torso of a frenzied maenad has been recognized as a reduced copy of Scopas' maenad, famous in the ancient world. The thin chiton has come open through the violent movement and gives a glimpse of the powerful, strained body.

Washing hair, pelike. The lady crouching down is having her hair washed by two serving women. While one of them pours water over her long hair, which falls forward, the other holds a towel ready for drying.

Serving maid at sacrifice, known as the girl from Antium. The young girl with hair loosely knotted over the brow makes preparations for a cult ritual.

Crouching Aphrodite. The goddess of love looks backwards into a mirror which Eros holds up to her. Her voluptuous body is very realistically presented, as Hellenistic taste required.

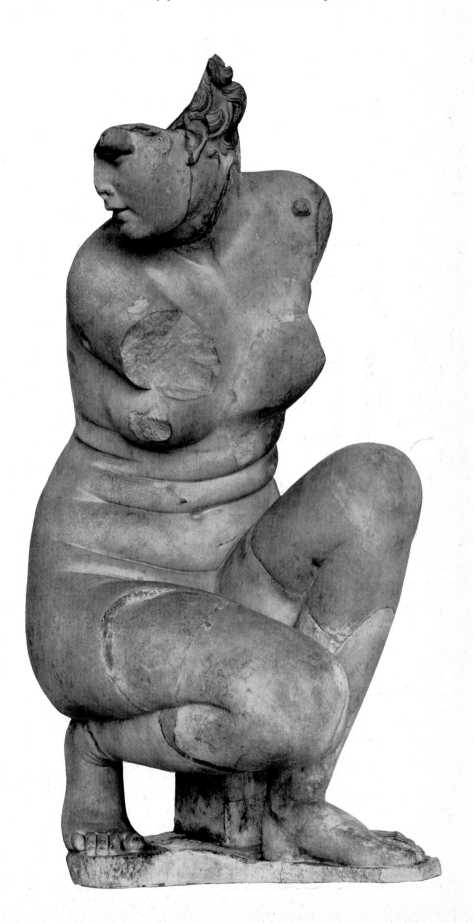

Terracotta statuette of a dancer in short skirt.

Terracotta statuette. The beautiful "Tanagra lady" is wrapped in a voluminous cloak, which she has drawn over her head. In addition she wears a flat, pointed hood. Her fan and the rich golden trimming on her gown betray the elegant lady.

Niobe and her youngest daughter. Niobe is punished by Apollo and Artemis because she had insulted their mother, Leto, out of an overweening pride in her own twelve children. The youngest daughter flees to Niobe's bosom, but is unable to escape her cruel fate.

Statue of Nicoclea, priestess of Demeter. The pedestal bears the following inscription: Nicoclea, daughter of Nicochorus, wife of Apollophanus, a gift to Demeter and Kore and the gods with Demeter.

71

This diadem of blossoms must have belonged to a rich lady. The ancient world loved jewelry; the precious metals were reserved for the upper classes, the ordinary women contenting themselves with cheaper materials like bronze, iron and amber.

Statue of woman, known as the little woman of Herculaneum. This figure wrapped in a voluminous cloak is thought to be the copy of a late work by Praxiteles or one of his school. She has her hair parted in what was known as the "melon" style: the whole head is striped with partings, the strands of hair being gathered at the back.

73

Nurse and child, terracotta from Myrina. A woman in calf-length chiton and cloak fondles a child.

Women at cult of the dead, from an amphora. Two serving girls tend their departed (?) mistress. The mirror, fan, sunshade and smart, brightly coloured robes make a contrast with the seriousness of looks and gestures.

The famous Venus of Milo. The particular charm of the work lies in the contrast between exposure and concealment. The cloak has slipped down to the hips but Aphrodite, unaware of her nudity, has her gaze fixed on the distance.

Aphrodite and Pan. This is a genre scene typical of Hellenistic art. Aphrodite, the goddess of love, confronts the lustful, goat's-footed Pan with flirtatious resistance. She threatens her importunate suitor with her sandal—but the small, winged Eros points to the end of the game.

Drunken old woman. The emaciated, sinewy old woman crouches down, clutching a large wine bottle to her bosom. The gown of heavy material leaves the right shoulder exposed. The head lolls drunkenly backward, the eyes stare emptily upwards, and a drunken stammering seems to come from the open mouth.

Fighting goddess. Detail from Pergamum altar. The struggle between the Gods of Olympus and the sons of earth, the Giants, is portrayed on the almost 120 m long frieze of this altar.

Aphrodite statuette. A cloak covers the love-goddess' naked body. It exposes the right breast and fits closely over body and thighs. The goddess wears a diadem in her centrally parted hair, while an armband encircles the upper left arm.

Greek goddesses: Athena, Hera, Aphrodite, Artemis, Nike,
Demeter, Hecate, and Hestia. In addition to these Olympic
goddesses the Greeks worshipped numerous other local and
lesser significant female deities.

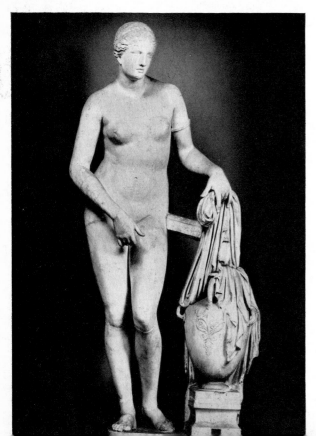

83

Etruscan clay sarcophagus. The deceased couple recline, as in life, on a sofa for a meal. Only the upper parts of their bodies, carefully clothed and turned towards the viewer, are realistically fashioned, while the lower parts lie flat and unsubstantial.

Crude realism: an Etruscan married couple on the lid of a burial urn.

A Roman married couple with the names *Aiedius and Aiedia* appear together on their tombstone relief.

Roman girl with parted hair. Terracotta from Latium.

87

Portrait of an old Roman woman.

The imperial family is portrayed participating in a procession to the altar of peace of Augustus in Rome. Clothed in voluminous robes, men, women and children walk to the dedication of the monument.

Apotheosis of the Empress Sabina. This relief decorated the marble monument to Sabina, Hadrian's wife. In the presence of the Emperor a torch-bearing spirit holds up the deified Sabina.

Vestal Virgin. As a sign of her priestly rank a woollen band is wrapped six times round her head, its ends hanging down over her shoulders. Over the back of her head she has laid the suffibulum, reaching to the shoulders, which is fastened on the breast with a brooch.

Little Roman girl with page-boy bob.

Young woman with writing materials. The beautiful young woman appears to the viewer in all the seriousness of concentrated meditation. She holds her pencil to her lips as a prelude to using the wax-covered writing tablet. Her curly hair is covered with a golden net and large golden rings hang from her ears.

Hair-styling was one of the main parts of a Roman lady's toilette. In the course of time the simplicity of central parting, knots and thick plaits such as we still find on Livia and Octavia, were abandoned and replaced by complicated coiffures. For such artistic "constructions" the ladies needed hairdressers who used hair-pieces and wigs for their creations.

 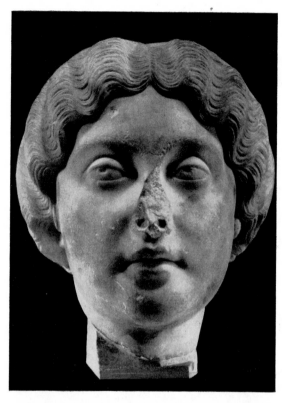 

Terentius Neo with wife, fresco. This double portrait shows Terentius Neo and his wife, who, sunk in thought, is holding pencil and
wax tablet. He holds a sealed roll of manuscript.

Sacrificial scene, relief. Sacrifice to Cybele with flute player and
drummer. An old woman approaches the altar and sprinkles grains of
incense on the fire. The two musicians play the exciting strains of the
Cybele cult.

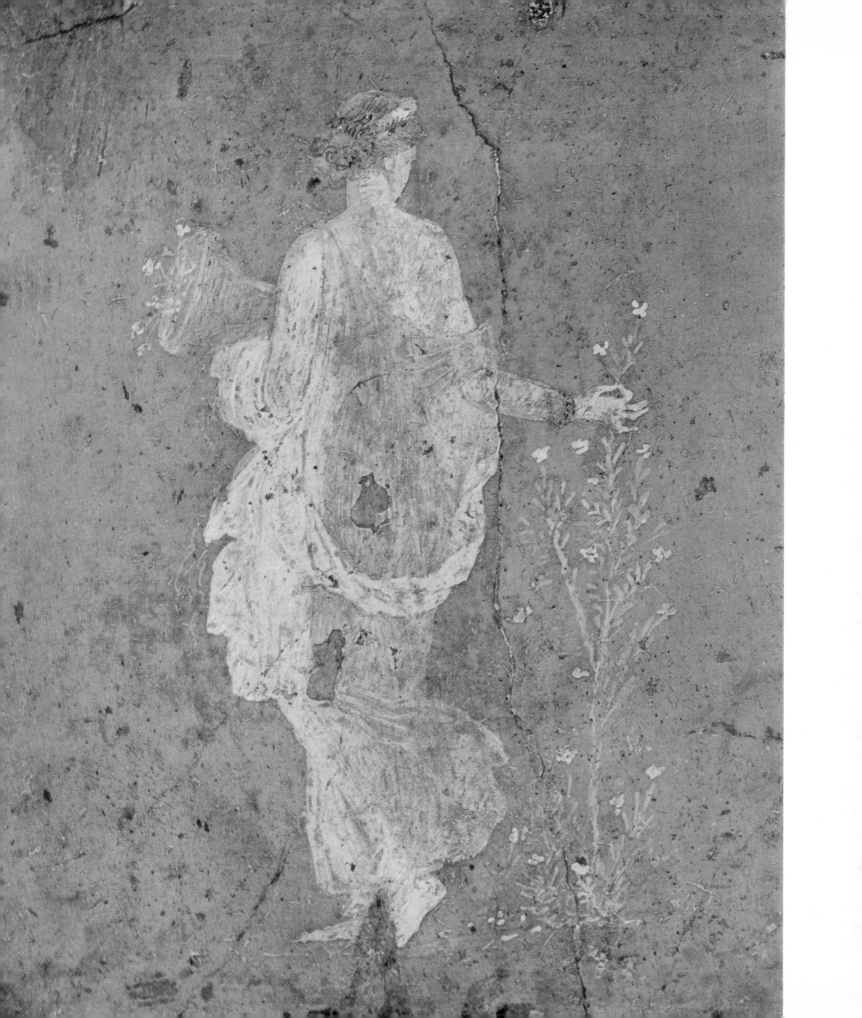

"*Spring,*" *fresco. This flower-girl breaks a bloom in passing.*

"*Aldobrandian wedding,*" *fresco. The nervous bride, clad all in white, sits anxiously on the marriage bed. Aphrodite or Peitho, the goddess of persuasion, concerns herself affectionately with her. Hymenaeus lurks expectantly on the step of the bridal chamber, while relatives and serving-maids prepare the wedding bath.*

Lady at toilette. An older lady has taken a seat in a cane armchair, placing her feet comfortably on a foot-stool. Four serving maids, their hair piled up in plaited crowns, attend to her: one has loosened her hair, two bring jugs and a fourth holds a mirror up to her.

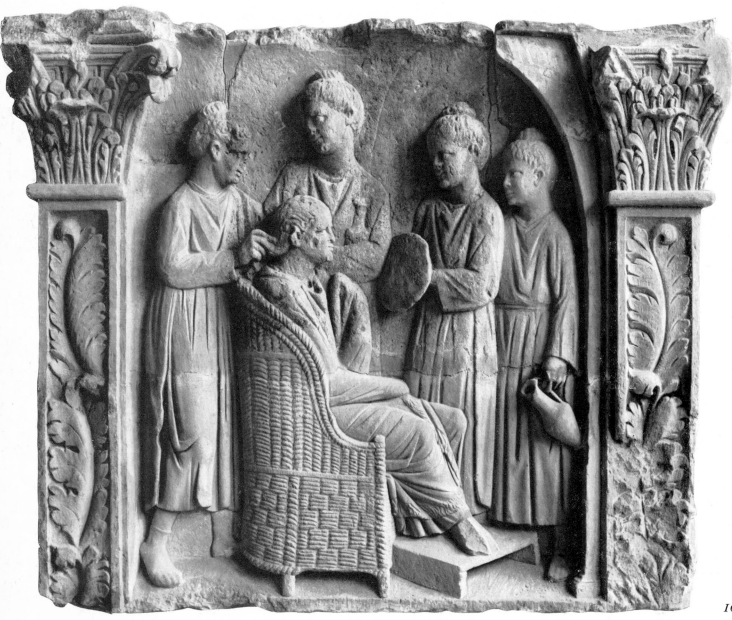

Make-up casket of ivory and metal.

Roman relief. A matron lies with her child—surrounded by her pets—upon a sofa and is served by a negress.

Woman combing herself, wall frieze from Pompeii. Eros holds the
mirror for this serious beauty. Perhaps she is a bride preparing her
hair for her wedding.

Women at a cult action, wall frieze from Pompeii. This scene is the first in a large frieze representing the unveiling of the holy phallus in the cult of Dionysus.

"Love-scene". This little mosaic gives a glimpse of the equipment of a Roman bedroom. The bed supported on four posts has a base of leather straps, a mattress on top and a cover which overhangs.

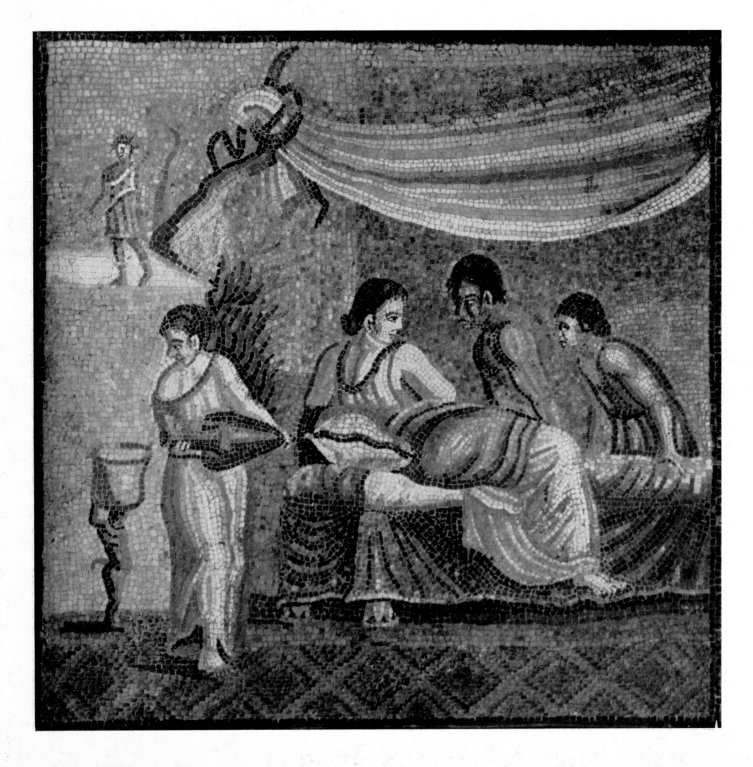

Lovers. Erotic portrayals are to be found everywhere in Roman art.

Girl athletes, mosaic from Sicily. These "bikini" girls show an astonishing state of undress. They appear in the arena clad only in brassière and loincloth.

Isis Cult Procession, marble relief. A priestess of Isis, lotus flower on brow, walks at the head of the procession. She holds the situla, a small vessel with handle. The holy Uraeus snake winds around her left arm. She is followed by a scribe with a book-roll, a priest in a wide cloak, carrying the holy water, and a young girl, her robe wound into Isis knots, bearing in her hands the sistrum and a ladle for the holy water.

Woman pouring perfume. Fresco from Villa Farnesina, in Rome. The young woman wears a double-girdled chiton and is veiled.

Toilette articles. Ivory combs, onyx flasks, glass bottles for perfume, etc. were some of the cosmetic aids of a Roman lady.

Mars and Venus. Empress Faustina the Younger appears as Venus in the society of the god Mars, who also has individual features.

Wedding sarcophagus. In the presence of allegorical personifications a couple give one another their hands. Behind them stands Concordia, harmony. Personifications of the senate, the Portus Romae (the Roman harbour) and of Annona (the state grain agency), of Ceres and Africa indicate the social position of the deceased, upon whose sarcophagus the wedding ceremony is portrayed. He was most probably prefect of Rome's grain distributing organization.

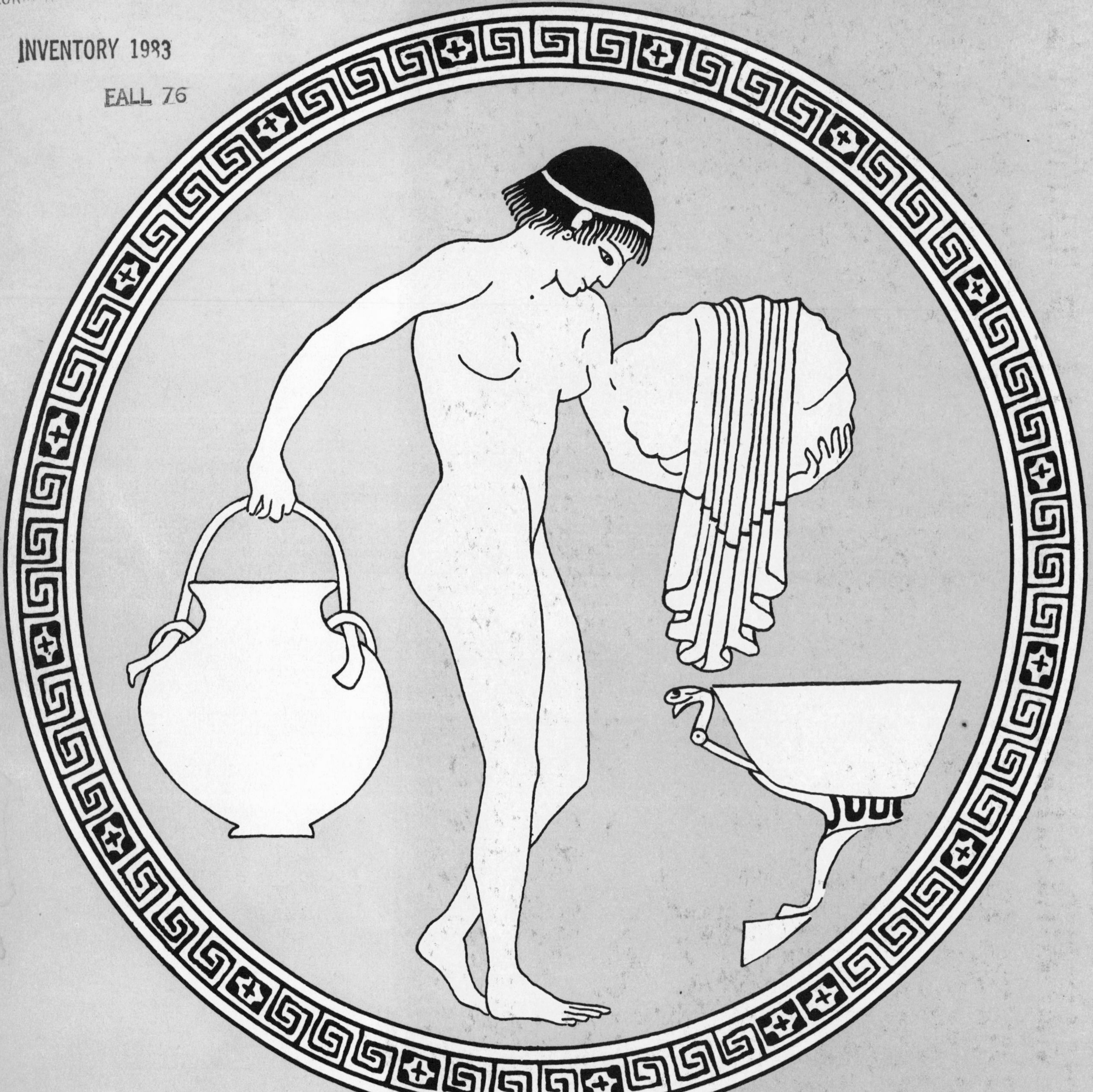